Daniel Has
Autism

Our Story of a Life Unexpected

Told by Kirsty & Michael Runnicles

ISBN 978-0-9954724-0-2

Published by Autism by Design

Hello

2007 – That was the year Autism formally introduced itself into our lives. Of course, it had been there for a lot longer but the subtle differences had largely failed to make any significant impact on our lives with our toddler son and baby daughter...but there had been niggles. So when we found ourselves in the paediatrician's office following a referral for our son, Daniel, the diagnosis of Autism came as both a shock and a revelation.

Over the years that has changed and now Autism features heavily in our daily lives. However, we are just a typical family of five, one son, two daughters, mum and dad.

Working parents with no expertise in managing a lifelong learning disability that accompanies our son's Autism diagnosis. Ultimately you have to learn on the job.

So back in 2007 we started out with newly diagnosed Autism by researching it and then by living, breathing and challenging it. Within this book, we are sharing our experience of living with Autism in the hope that it challenges some of the misplaced preconceptions that exist and also highlights the need for better understanding of a very complex condition.

It was and still is, a journey into the unknown and we are still finding our way.

Daniel

Please meet Daniel, age 11. Daniel was diagnosed with Autism, aged 2 when it became clear that he wasn't hitting certain developmental milestones. He has been teaching us all about Autism ever since.

Daniel is known for his cheeky smile and infectious giggle. He is non-verbal but has his own unique vocalisation and will often greet you with an 'Ey'. A Jekyll and Hyde character who can go from tears to laughter in minutes and every emotion in between. Daniel challenges the stereotypes of Autism whilst ticking every box at the same time.

Daniel loves nothing more than to bounce on his trampoline, all year round whatever the weather. When we really have to say 'no' to outside play, he can usually be found pairing objects. Give him two of anything and he can be occupied for hours. Deviate from the unspoken rule book and you will find yourself under the wrath of Daniel.

Mike & Kirsty

Our story began in 2002 when we met one very wet and stormy evening at a local pub. We are both typically shy and quiet and so striking up conversations with someone new could have been awkward. Fortunately, it wasn't and the perfect love story started right there.

In 2004, as newlyweds, we were keen to start a family and later that same year were blessed with our first born Daniel. He was, as he is now, a beautiful child and for the first few years, life carried on with no real anticipation for the journey ahead.

Like for most people, our lives revolved our family, friends and jobs. Mike is a keen aviation enthusiast where as I am a lifelong Michael Jackson fan.

We have to point out that neither of us were newcomers to disability. Both had parents who had Multiple Sclerosis, an auto-immune condition affecting the brain. However, Autism was a completely new minefield and it quickly became clear that there was no-one to guide us through it.

Rebecca & Sophie

Rebecca, age 9 and Sophie, age 6 are Daniel's younger sisters. When these two are not bickering with each other, they are whirlwinds of creativity and imaginative play. Rebecca is very much the leader and Sophie tends to go with the flow.

Both have never experienced life without Autism and for the most part take in their stride.

They both act as extra pairs of eyes by understanding that Daniel needs supervision in everything he does and will (usually) take on this role with enthusiasm if we have to momentarily leave the room. That isn't to say that Autism doesn't impact them and they openly admit to sometimes feeling scared of Daniel when he is midst meltdown or frustrated that they cannot do things as freely as others, have friends over as example.

On the whole though both girls are extremely resilient and accepting of the situation which is a life lesson that may be valuable in the future.

Dedication

The biggest inspiration for this book is Daniel for giving us insight into the world of Autism and for being the unique, beautiful young man that he is. Equally, Daniel's siblings Rebecca and Sophie without whom our world would be a darker place.

We would also like to thank our close family and friends for supporting us through some pretty harrowing times, wiping away our tears and laughing with us in the brighter moments. We recognise that it hasn't been an easy road for those around us and we are eternally grateful for all the times you have stepped in to help.

We are also indebted to a huge number of individuals that have come into our lives as a direct result of Autism. Professionals, Carers, Respite Providers and new found friends within the Autism community. Each and every one has touched our lives and we could dedicate pages to them. Hopefully you all know who you are.

A shout out to:

Ebony and Lisa, for going above and beyond the call of duty and giving us much needed respite in some of Daniel's darker moments.

Kangaroos – for your continued support but particularly in recognition for the summer of 2015, where Daniel was allowed to 'carry on as normal' whilst facing new medical challenges that prevented him doing so elsewhere.

Finally, we would like to thank the team at The Other Publishing Company for supporting us and believing in us enough to see this through to fruition.

Daniel Has Autism

Our Story of a Life Unexpected

.

Baby Makes Three

As it turned out, my expanding waistline wasn't just a result of the wedding buffet.

March 25th 2004... a day filled with the most wonderfully diverse mixture of feelings: shock, fear but more significantly extreme happiness. Those two blue lines on the pregnancy stick indicated only one thing. As newlyweds, we were about to experience another life changing event in approximately 8 months' time.

I am sure that the "bean", "alien", "bump" encountered a number of nicknames through the three trimesters, but one thing was for sure, this baby was loved from the minute we knew of his/her existence. Like many first time parents, our reading material altered to be anything and everything baby related.

Pregnancy progressed without any major issues. There was an initial scare in the early days where I experienced some worrying cramps so had an early scan at seven weeks. The statistics for miscarriage were imprinted in my mind so I recall feeling massive relief at seeing a little heart beating away.

Besides that, the inside of a toilet bowl became my friend for the first few months. I had gone from an all you can eat buffet (our honeymoon in Barbados) to a handful of ginger biscuits, dry toast and crackers within a matter of weeks. In the latter months pelvic girdle pain set in and my transformation, complete with penguin waddle, was made. We followed the week-by-week guides of 'what to expect', and regimentally attended the antenatal appointments with the midwife to make sure baby was thriving.

Prior to pregnancy, I had rarely set foot in hospital other than to either visit or accompany others. But first pregnancies involve a lot of health checks, routine blood tests and ultrasound scans. I'll admit to having been more than a little anxious at the prospect that something could go wrong, so I relished these appointments, like a sponge, absorbing all the information as we went. We had a home Doppler device that picks up sound waves, and this allowed us to regularly check on baby's heartbeat.

At our twenty-week ultrasound appointment we were keen to find out whether baby was a boy or girl... A BOY! Even more fantastic was the news that no anomalies were evident and all vital organs were present.

Nesting took over from about thirty weeks as I started to prepare for the arrival of our son. This little being was our everything and everything had to be perfect for him. That unconditional love had been there from the start. Autism was very much an unknown and didn't relate to us. It had no place in our lives at that point. It isn't something that you read about in parenting books; well, certainly not in relation to antenatal care or the first twelve months of life. Besides anything else, you have to get past the birth before you really take on board what parenthood means!

From Here to Paternity

Birth Day... or is it?

I suppose if I'd known we were on the cusp of entering a period of such intense activity, the dawn of a new existence as a "family", rather than just a married couple, a fundamental change in our whole way of life and very existence, I might have rolled over and had an extra hour or two in bed that Saturday morning.

As things were, Kirsty had only commenced her maternity leave the previous Friday, and we knew the due date was still nearly two weeks away – the 1st December, but I had also been comprehensively convinced – not just by one, but by many supposedly "knowledgeable" colleagues and parents, that first babies always drag things out as long as possible. I had more or less resigned myself to enduring hours, days and weeks dragging by, as I sat in the office clutching my mobile phone, awaiting "the call". To make things worse, a series of major road re-surfacing works along virtually every road on the industrial estate was due to kick off imminently, at the worst possible time. The call would come, I just knew it, right as the afternoon rush hour built up to a peak of complete static congestion. I would depart the office a nervous wreck and immediately find myself confined in a queue of traffic.

Fortunately, as things turned out, I need not have worried. In fact, events turned so quickly that weekend that I don't think either of us even had the time to start the proper worrying "build up" phase!

Back at home, and Kirsty was suffering from contractions increasing in severity. "Real ones or very strong Braxton Hicks?" was without doubt the question on our minds. This, combined with a comparative lack of perceived movement by the bump, soon prompted our first call to the maternity department, where they felt it wise that we come in and get Kirsty looked at. Wow! Another adrenaline surge, much bigger... Could this be it, could this be the big event?! There followed what can only be described as "calm and fairly relaxed panic stations" as we prepared ourselves and strapped into the car for the cross-country drive. Labour bag? Check... Baby's bag? Check... Baby car seat fitted? Check... and we were on our way.

A real sense of excitement, fear and trepidation was abundant in my mind as we entered the maternity department. The staff there swiftly and efficiently ushered us into a delivery suite, where we stood awaiting impending action stations. Someone would come in, carry out some kind of check or examination, and we'd know where we were and what to expect in the coming hours... or so I thought. Perhaps all first time fathers feel this, I don't know. I soon realised that the term "action stations" was far from the reality that followed.

Fast forward several hours and our hopes were raised when the next midwife stated that she felt that contractions and possibly even initial signs of labour were definitely underway. Yet, despite all our efforts, our baby remained stubbornly opposed to moving, and no obvious progression was evident. We were now well into the small hours of the morning, and both suffering from serious tiredness.

A short while later, the next in the long line of hospital midwives that night came in, a slightly older and clearly very experienced lady called Ivy. Ivy performed her own assessment there and then, and stated in no uncertain terms that Kirsty was not in labour or due to give birth at any time in the immediate future. Kirsty would be given some pain relief to ease the contraction pains and help her to sleep, whilst I would return home by myself and catch some much needed sleep there.

So, at some time close to 4am on Sunday morning, I summoned up my remaining energy and hit the road.

Birth Day

And Breathe...

I awoke to the bright morning daylight, just a few hours later that Sunday – still feeling somewhat groggy, but a lot more refreshed than I had felt for some while! There had not – at least to my knowledge – been any urgent calls from hospital but I made tracks back to the delivery suite.

On arrival, I entered to find Kirsty washed and dressed, and clearly more refreshed than when I had left – and above all else, still very, very pregnant! It was decided that the best thing would be for her to return home, and come back to the hospital only when regular contractions commenced again. So about 30 minutes later we found ourselves unexpectedly back to square one – at home together, waiting for our little bundle to arrive.

The day passed by rather strangely and serenely for the first few hours as I recall. By the early evening, the contractions were now recommencing but we had made plans to pop over to family briefly and decided to carry on with this. I could see from her expression that the pain from each contraction was growing, and eventually we politely made our excuses and made for home around 8pm. Unbeknown to me, even as we said our goodbyes and walked to the car, Kirsty's waters were breaking.

Back home again, and both the nerves and adrenalin surge had returned to both of us. After a brief interlude we collected the hospital bags and prepared for the night ahead. Unusually, Kirsty was seated in the back of the car as we set off for hospital – the rationale being that she could stretch out and move around to find the most comfortable position, although this was clearly becoming more difficult with every second that passed. Despite the pain, Kirsty was still capable of some clear thought – and asked me whether I could recall picking up the maternity notes folder... and immediately dealt me a severe hammer blow! "OH ****!" I thought. In the last minute to leave, I had not picked up the clear plastic folder on the coffee table. Probably the second most important item after remembering to load Kirsty herself into the car. My mind raced... surely they could survive in the delivery suite without a few bits of paper in a folder.

Arriving back at hospital, Kirsty made it clear she was suffering. I think this time around staff realised that things might be on the move, as we were fairly swiftly shown to a delivery suite. Then, to the relief of both of us, the first midwife to enter was Ivy, seemingly the most knowledgeable of the line-up from the previous night. Relief soon turned to panic, however – not due to any imminent medical problem. This time I was the one in trouble, for forgetting to pick up Kirsty's pregnancy notes when leaving the house! Ivy was adamant that these notes were absolutely essential for the delivery of our baby. In fact, the impression was given that our situation was nigh on completely hopeless without them. It almost seemed like the whole hospital would fail to function, and we would be sent home and everything shut down if a way could not be found to get the pregnancy notes there immediately. By now, I was feeling rather like a school boy who's been severely told off by a towering, intimidating headmaster! Fortunately, expectant grandparents were on hand to deliver the notes – the first of many grandparent duties.

The following seconds... or was it minutes... or was it hours... passed by painfully (and I don't mean painfully slow or painfully quickly... just painfully, for Kirsty!). To be honest, I was not even aware of the absolute passage of time at all. Kirsty endured the intensifying contractions as they came and went, and each time I could feel her tense up and deeply inhale the gas and air mixture to try to find any relief possible. There was precious little I could do, except remain by her side, hold her hand and give whatever verbal encouragement I could provide. This was to prove a difficult time for me... Yes, I know I was not in any physical pain or discomfort myself, but the emotional pain of watching my wife suffer intense pain – to see it coming each time, and be able to DO NOTHING to stop or relieve it, was often excruciating. Somehow I did my level best to suppress any evidence of this, and I think I succeeded – although at times I will admit being close to tears.

Up until this point, Kirsty had coped admirably with the pain levels, with nothing other than the TENS machine and Entonox gas. It began to look likely she'd make it through without the further relief of pethidine or an epidural. As it turned out, though, the worst was yet to come... in the form of very intense back pains. This transpired because of our baby's positioning in the womb. Normally, a baby should be positioned facing head-down and facing the mother's back. Our baby boy, however, had decided that he wanted a forward facing view for his arrival into the outside world. This forward facing position was responsible for severe pain in Kirsty's back during delivery, which kicked in with a vengeance when the pushing started.

So, the minutes passed, and Ivy and I offered all the encouragement we could. Our baby was close – very close –to arriving, but couldn't quite make it. The pain and effort were by now beginning to take their toll on Kirsty, and tiredness started to creep in. This seemed to be re-ducing the strength of each contraction and pushing force at exactly the time when the biggest efforts were needed.

After some time of this, Ivy conceded that further action was need-ed and a doctor was called to deliver our baby by ventouse. A ventouse is basically a device which is applied to the baby's head, and then held

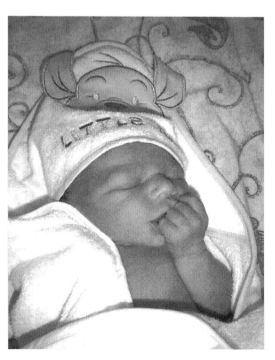

in position by suction, al-lowing the doctor or mid-wife to help pull the baby during each contraction. To our relief, the doctor arrived promptly and be-gan the procedure.

So, with the doctor working at the "business end" alongside Ivy, and me providing as much encouragement as possi-ble, after just a few more contractions I saw the most miraculous sight imaginable – our little boy's head had emerged into the world for the first time! All I remember seeing is this perfect little face right there! Time seemed to freeze for just that instant – then sud-denly there was a blur of activity. Within moments our baby was born, then the umbilical cord was cut without my even noticing and we both heard this wonderful cry as he took his first breaths of air.

Within a few more seconds, Daniel was wrapped in a towel and placed on Kirsty's tummy for us to see and talk to for the first time... and I enjoyed the most wonderful moment of holding my baby son for the first time...

Milestone Amiss

From the minute we are born, targets are placed upon our heads.

Those early months were again a mix of shock, fear and extreme happiness with the added touch of sleep deprivation thrown in. Our little boy was perfect, beautiful chubby tiny fingers and toes and miniature features, gloriously pink after a feed, full bellied, snuggled contently just like a piglet, a nickname he holds to this day.

Daniel had and still has the most infectious smile. As new parents we noticed nothing out of the ordinary. Everything we had been told to expect – sleepless nights, colic, toxic nappies – held us in good stead. Around 12 months of age, our piglet had developed into a 'babble-bottom' reciting tunes from nursery rhymes and the occasional dada, mummm, bye bye. At fifteen months his favourite word was "bugger" which all found amusing but no-one will admit to its origin.

Babbling disappeared as quickly as it arrived and no real language has developed since. We have a very vocal little boy but not all sounds are easy on the ear and are far removed from the cuteness of toddlerhood.

Parenting books – well, we had followed them religiously through pregnancy and the newborn stages. Often they had sections about ongoing development and the toddler years. Yet in our newly established family, we were taking one day at a time and didn't dwell too much on the 'later' milestones such as talking. Daniel was hitting his early milestones without issue so we had no real reason to expect that these things wouldn't come with time. Indeed, when we first raised concerns it was very much made clear by family and friends that we were just being over-anxious first time parents.

However, much like all things to do with your child, when you know... only *you* know! For a time after that, prior to official diagnosis, those milestones became a noose around our necks. We were painfully aware of them and whilst we tried to help Daniel as much as we could, he was amidst regression so was losing skills at a greater rate than attaining them.

Daniel was a late walker. I can remember stressing that he was never going to get past a bottom shuffle. His little sister Rebecca was on the way, due within months, then weeks. Fifteen months passed by, speedy on all fours. Sixteen months passed by, the occasional stand

up against furniture. Seventeen months arrived, within two weeks of Rebecca's arrival and he was up. He hasn't looked back since and possesses strong gross motor skills and a good set of leg muscles that you need to worry about if he breaks out into a sprint. Yet for a while, you know that was a concern.

You panic when your child isn't doing something that all their peers are doing. You question, you doubt, your raise your hopes, hopes are diminished and so the cycle continues.

Typically a child will be subject to development checks by physicians and other child health professionals. In the UK, a health visitor will monitor a child's progress from newborn until the age of five. A health visitor is a qualified nurse or midwife who has undertaken further training to specialise in this area of child development. They will look at a child's growth, health and development and be on hand to offer advice.

Social skills form part of these development checks and it is expected that children will reach certain milestones in their formative years. It is often when a child is deemed not to have met these milestones that further assessment is suggested, but not always. It is important to remember that every child is different and that milestones are guidelines only.

For some individuals on the autistic spectrum, their difficulties may not become apparent until after they start school. At this point concerns may be raised with the teacher, GP/Physician or school nurse who may be able to refer for further assessment. However, autism is a complex condition that is not fully understood and concerns raised by parents may not be shared in other settings. There is nothing worse than being made to feel like a neurotic parent. However, parents' concerns should never be dismissed.

Daniel has many more milestones to hit. We don't know if they will be met. What we have learnt is that there isn't a time limit for them and they don't govern life. You also need to find the positive sometimes, however difficult that might be. If a task seems impossible and looks like it is never going to happen, break it down into bite size pieces and tackle one at a time. Ultimately we will continue to push Daniel to achieve his very best, but not by forsaking what he has already. Sometimes life is taken over by the 'what ifs' and not enough thought is given to the 'what is'.

A Daddy Looking Back –Initial Diagnosis

Part 1

Even though it was expected, hearing it out loud left the words swimming around in my head. What does it actually mean?

I suppose that any thoughts discussing my son's autism really ought to start when the autism started. But now, there's an impossible thought – how would I know when it started? Was it always there perhaps, lurking in the background? Or did it appear suddenly, when we weren't looking? Autism defies objective identification. There is no 'test' that confirms its appearance, at least not today. You won't see two doctors holding up an X-ray or scan image, deep in discussion, pointing to distinctive markers before nodding their heads in unison, one stating "It's autism" with the other shortly afterward saying "I concur." There's no positive or negative lab result. As far as I can tell, it's a totally subjective and very "hit and miss" assessment by a paediatrician based purely on certain behavioural patterns (or the lack of) and missed milestones in development.

That's the other thing... It creeps up on you. It doesn't hit you like a hammer blow or a broken bone. You don't wake up and find your son one day has, overnight, become severely autistic with significant developmental delays. As far as we were aware, he started off in life just fine. Sure, he was a little awkward at birth, lying "back to back" with his mum and requiring the assistance of a ventouse to make his entrance – but nothing unusual. Like most babies we had bouts of colic and sleepless nights, but all normal. There are plenty of photos of our beautiful son beaming at the camera, crawling around, exploring, being mischievous and generally all the things we would ever want our much-loved baby boy to do. He was a little late walking, but he got there in the end. And whilst speech seemed to be late making an entrance, there were signs of babbling. The expected attempts at Mumma, Dadda, Doggy, and a very good try at the theme tune to children's TV show "Balamory" all made an appearance, albeit quite late. Sure, we had concerns, but nothing I wouldn't expect all parents to have where their child's development is concerned. It can be heart-breaking to think back to all of these things now.

So where did it all go wrong? Did we miss something early that could have prevented the inexorable slide towards the diagnosis? It's an emotional and not an easy subject to discuss... Daniel had the usual vaccinations, including the "proven to be 100% safe" MMR jab. Did that have anything to do with it? Sure, how could we not have doubts given so much publicity? Daniel had a skin condition, treated at length with repeated prescriptions of antibiotics. Did they have anything to do with it? There is no way we can possibly know! Did he already have it from birth, some minor defect hidden away, triggered at some stage of his brain's development? At this point in time I tend to think maybe he was genetically pre-disposed to develop autism, however *not* guaranteed to get it. Some external trigger or agent, maybe a vaccination, maybe a chemical he encountered, maybe the antibiotics or something completely different, something I've heard termed as an "insult" to his body, tipped things over the edge. These days it's best not to dwell too much on what we might have done differently. It will kill you every time to look back and think "if only we'd done this..." and achieves nothing.

So, Daniel lost his few words and lost the babbling. We noticed he would not beam at you and look at your eyes when you played with him. He'd stare blankly into space from his highchair, sometimes appearing to look straight through you into space. He wouldn't really play with toys in the usual way, instead holding them up and waving them, examining them, but not really playing in the usual sense with them.

Life went on... Then the wonderful news that we were expecting a second child in May 2006, just eighteen months after Daniel was born. Looking back, although not specifically planned that soon, this was unknowingly a fantastic stroke of good fortune. It's difficult to say what choices we may have made had our son's diagnosis occurred before then, and whether or not we would have tried for a second child. But arrive she did, in determined style and far more rapid fashion than her older brother! I couldn't have felt more proud to now be a Daddy to a wonderful son and daughter. By this time however, and thinking back it's clear that Daniel's difficulties were still evident. On our first little family break away to a holiday park in Dorset in September 2006, we almost returned home before unpacking, after an extreme and unexpected bout of distress around the moment we arrived. Thankfully we didn't and had a wonderful time together on that holiday and plenty of laughs.

However, in early spring 2007, with our son now some 27 months old and showing little significant further development, came the fateful review with Daniel's paediatrician. The diagnosis we had already braced ourselves for – our son was "officially" on the autistic spectrum. He was exactly the same the day before... and the same the day after... except for the diagnosis. Not that we knew it at the time, but the roller-coaster of life for us really launched at that point!

So... the opening chapter in our life with autism. When my wife Kirsty read these thoughts, she expressed concern about the heavy nature of them. *"There's that word again – heavy. Is there a problem with the Earth's gravitational field in the future?"* I guess it's true. Whilst there are plenty of topics that will celebrate the joys, the laughs and more light-hearted aspects of life with our son – in this instance, it's difficult to be anything other than honest about a difficult time.

So What Is It?

Ask the question to a number of people either on the spectrum or who have loved ones on it and you'll find that the answer may not always be the same.

The film 'Rain Man' centres on a character, Raymond played by Dustin Hoffman, who has autism. However, if you went up to a carer or family member of someone on the autistic spectrum and said, 'oh so and so is like Dustin Hoffman in Rain Man', you are likely to be met with a heavy sigh. Rain Man did a very good job of bringing autism to the general public's attention and Raymond was quickly adopted as the most popular stereotype for autism. Sadly, it is a misconception as very few individuals on the spectrum present like Raymond. Whilst some people do have genius or savant abilities, they are very rare and these traits hide the real struggles they typically face.

The word 'autism' originates from the Greek word 'autos', meaning self or by oneself. The term describes someone being absorbed within oneself.

Autism was a term first used by Eugen Bleuler, a Swiss psychiatrist, in 1911 to refer to one group of symptoms of schizophrenia. Historically the two conditions have been closely linked although more recent research has defined them as two separate conditions.

Leo Kanner is a doctor who is credited for correctly using the term 'autism' in 1943 to be what we recognise it as today.

Hans Asperger was an Austrian paediatrician who provided the definition of Asperger's Syndrome, a condition that appears on the autistic spectrum. It is often considered to be on the higher functioning end of the spectrum.

Autism is a lifelong developmental disability that affects the way a person communicates and relates to people around them. Autism is considered to be on a spectrum, meaning that the impairments range from mild to severe. Whilst it is true that all individuals on the spectrum require support from others to overcome their difficulties, some will go on to live fully independently whilst others will require a lifetime of care to ensure they are kept safe and well.

To be diagnosed with autism you need to present with difficulties in the following areas:

Social Interaction – Examples of impairment include inability to make eye contact, little or no understanding of visual cues such as facial expressions or inappropriate reactions such as laughing if someone cries.

Social Communication – Difficulties in using either verbal or non-verbal communication methods to express needs or to be receptive to communication used by others.

Imagination – Unable to role play, lack of empathy towards other, repetitive.

This is known as the triad of impairments.

For a person to be diagnosed with autism, they must experience difficulties in all of these areas. However, the impairment varies from person to person and no two individuals with autism may present the same. So whilst we cannot discount Raymond in Rain Man as a valid example of someone living with autism, the facts are that the variations are too great to stereotype.

Autism organisations can provide a wealth of information and support. They are often equipped with helplines or forums that allow you to talk through or discuss your concerns or be put in touch with experts, parents or carers and other organisations.

In the US: www.autism-society.org
In the UK: www.autism.org.uk

"Houston, We've Had a Problem..." – Initial Diagnosis

Part 2

"We just lost the moon." Jim Lovell

Most people will know about the story of Apollo 13. Three astronauts, Jim Lovell, Fred Haise and Jack Swigert, speeding away from Earth, by now some two hundred thousand miles from home, when inexplicably it all went very wrong. Here's an interesting fact – that world famous line is nearly always misquoted as "Houston we *have* a problem". I've sometimes pondered in recent years whether the very fact that I know facts such as this, to what might be called a "nerdy" level of detail (combined with a 24-year career in software engineering), might indicate a possible genetic contributory factor to Daniel's autism... but I digress, and that is a subject for some other day!

Anyway, imagine the scene on board the Command Module Odyssey. "We've had a main bus B undervolt," states Lovell, continuing to report as further lights on the caution and warning panels illuminate like a Christmas tree. There's clearly a problem, a serious one, with the spacecraft. It's no longer working as it should, and the crew is in trouble. Their hopes and dreams of successfully entering lunar orbit, then piloting their Lunar Module Aquarius to the Fra Maura highlands on the surface of the moon, look to be in doubt. Their whole future suddenly appears to be in doubt.

Back in Mission Control in Houston, the support team listens to the grim news as more and more problems become evident. Finally, after several tense moments as Flight Controller Gene Kranz discusses the condition of the malfunctioning spacecraft, Capcom Jack Lousma contacts the three astronauts. "Odyssey, Houston... <pause> ...Really sorry to hear about the problems with the spacecraft... That's really tough... <pause> Good luck with that one, guys..." <click> ...silence.

Thankfully, this is not what happened to Apollo 13. However, if one replaces (and this is a stretch, but will make sense... honest) (i) the malfunctioning spacecraft with our son following his diagnosis of autism, (ii) the astronauts with us as parents, and (iii) Mission Control in Houston with the British National Health Service (NHS), suddenly the "modified scenario" described above gives some idea of how we felt in the immediate aftermath of Daniel's diagnosis. In short – the NHS does not attempt to treat autism. You are basically told "sorry" and "good luck with that" and sent on your way with a bunch of leaflets about support and assistance.

Let's imagine, continuing my modified story for a further moment, that our three astronauts eventually manage to bring their adrenaline levels under some limited control, calm themselves and re-group. With the limited on-board resources at their disposal, including various spacecraft manuals and checklists as well as their own extensive knowledge of the Command Module systems, Lovell, Haise and Swigert concoct some ideas that might help "treat" some of the damaged systems. Lovell radios Houston with their plan... And after a short pause, Jack Lousma comes back for a second time: "Uh, Jim, we think you're wasting your time on that one. Quite honestly that won't make any difference". Clearly not very helpful.

So, to sum up, the "official position" of the NHS is that autism is not a condition that can be treated, hence you shouldn't (unless you're lucky enough to have one of the very rare GPs who follow something called the "DAN" methodologies – where DAN = Defeat Autism Now") expect any NHS funded treatment to try to *combat* autism or cure it. (Many don't agree autism is something that should be treated in any case... but again, a topic for another day.) Partly because autism is really, still not fully understood by any stretch of the imagination in the first place. When researching online there are hundreds if not thousands of suggested treatments for autism – and many claims of improvements, benefits and even "miraculous cures". But as the saying goes with this particular condition, "If you've met one child with autism... You've met one child with autism". Sure, it's quite possible many of these treatments DO work with many kids, but equally most treatments don't work with many. The NHS is not in a position to fund dozens and dozens of expensive treatments in what would clearly be a complete lottery in a vague hope that a treatment does lead to improvement.

Still, at the time it did feel like we were cast adrift in outer space with no clue what to do...

BUT, for anyone reading this who may be in the same position as us... Despite no checklists, operations manuals or help from Houston, we are all still here, we've muddled through and continue to do so. The best advice, about as far away from the scientists and engineers at NASA as you could imagine, is summed up by Corporal Jones from Dad's Army. "Don't Panic! DON'T PANIC!" And know that there are others like you out there, more than you know...

Going Anywhere This Year?

We have searched endlessly for autism friendly breaks and some look wonderful but still, they somehow are not quite for Daniel.

In years gone by, as a fledgling couple both Mike and I were lucky to travel to various locations in the UK, Europe and further afield to Florida, Australia and Barbados. Indeed, with a baby Daniel, we managed a transatlantic break with very little effort.

It was September 2006 when we ventured to Hoburne Naish in Dorset for a short break in a lodge. Daniel was almost 2 years of age and Rebecca was 4 months. The lodge was a large dark wooden cabin and from the moment Daniel set his eyes on it he screamed. At this point, Daniel had not been diagnosed and I am not sure "autism" had even been mentioned. Anyway, Daniel appeared to be absolutely terrified of this large but actually very nice building we found ourselves in. The screaming continued constantly for hours with no relent. We went for a walk around the complex and he did calm down but as soon we ventured near "any" of these wooden scream-inducing structures, full-blown hysterics would occur. We seriously considered going home, sure that he was coming down with something. However, he eventually tired himself out and slept and was a little calmer the next day but we still experienced these episodes as he went in and out of the lodge.

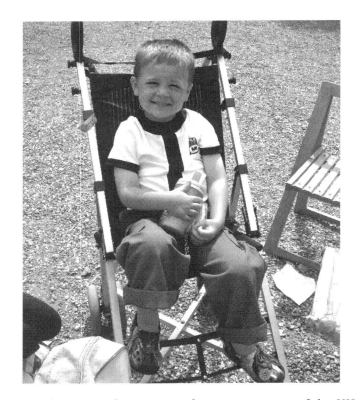

July 2007 and we were brave enough to venture out of the UK armed with little more than Medised, grandparents and aunty in tow, to Florida. It had been approximately four months since Daniel was diagnosed, and we advised the airline because we had no idea how Daniel would take to flying, conscious that he had become very nervous about new places. The flight wasn't disastrous and I wouldn't say our two were particularly troublesome during the time out there. However, Daniel's sleep patterns were awful and although at the time we put it down to jetlag and time difference, it was actually the start of an overall decline in sleep behaviour.

Goodbye Sleep

Part 1

Nothing really prepares you for how a prolonged period of sleep deprivation can make you feel.

On sharing the news that you are expecting a baby, the first gem of advice you are given is often 'Say goodbye to a good night's sleep'.

In those early days it is true, and the lack of sleep hits you like a bulldozer. The health visitor will tell you 'sleep when baby sleeps' and 'take it easy', which is all well and good but life doesn't stop just because you have had a baby.

If you are lucky, around 12 weeks baby may have settled into a sleeping pattern and possibly realized that night-time is for sleeping and not pooping and playtime. If you are lucky.

Daniel's sleep patterns did settle down at 12 weeks of age. He periodically suffered from bowel trouble and had fairly regularly disturbed sleep but it was manageable. As new parents we imagined that this was fairly typical and were still able to joke about saying goodbye to lie-ins.

Indeed, this pattern continued until about the age of 3.5 years when Daniel's sleeping patterns took a dramatic turn for the worse. Around this age we said goodbye to the daytime nap. We had moved house in December of 2007 and although he seemed to have dealt with the move reasonably well, it did herald the start of a noticeable change in diet preferences, a decline in mood and, more significantly, sleep issues.

Typically, Daniel would go to bed around 7pm, be quite content for maybe 30 minutes, long enough to get his little sister ready for bed, and then all hell would break loose. He would become extremely distressed very quickly and be completely inconsolable. As parents, we would take it in turns to sit with him trying to calm him. These sessions could go on until 10-11pm at night, before we finally managed to get him to settle.

This was not the end of the upset, though, and by 2am he was often awake again, sometimes for an hour, but often for the rest of the night. The summer months of 2008 were absolute hell.

Having decided to stay in the UK, we ventured to Center Parcs at Longleat. The first visit was quite successful but it was difficult to entertain Daniel and it became apparent that his danger awareness was zero. He didn't sleep very well whilst there but to a certain extent we put it down to the new environment and his age, still very much a toddler!

We decided to return in autumn 2008 but this time Daniel's behaviour was much worse and from what I remember he didn't sleep at all. We tried putting him in a room on his own but then noticed a curly lead attached to a hair dryer that could not be removed. In hindsight this was a hazard to any toddler but it was a focus whilst we tried to get him to settle. It did get to the point where we thought we might have to come home, with Daniel alternating between hyperactivity and extreme distress. Indeed, on the journey home, Daniel was tantruming in the car and hitting Rebecca to the point that we had to stop the car and separate them.

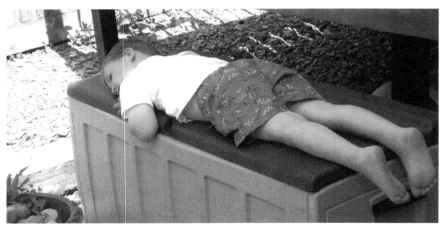

We were reaching the end of our tether, with severe sleep deprivation whilst trying to work full-time and look after two under-fives becoming incredibly challenging. It was time to seek outside help!

Boy vs Food

Daniel's eating habits go against the Holy Grail of Parenting Guides.

There is a lot of debate as to whether food contributes to autism in a 'you are what you eat' kind of way. A lot of research centres on gastrointestinal issues and the relationship with autism. Now, we have followed limited diets with Daniel and it is NOT easy and we have also followed bio-medical protocols, which is as overwhelming in practice as the jargon associated with it. The only vaguely amusing thing was that those practicing in biomedical interventions are affectionately known as 'DAN' doctors (Daniel: Dan get it?)... must get out more!

So, Daniel started off life as a breast-fed baby. Around four to five weeks, we started to introduce a bottle of formula. By about four months, it was at least one bottle daily. At five months Daniel started baby swimming and with it started to develop quite a nasty case of eczema. Unbeknown to us at the time, the rash was most likely contributed to by the formula milk and not the swimming. Fast forward a further few months and weaning, Daniel suffered awful tummy aches and although the swimming class had finished, the eczema continued to cover him in an ugly rash. By this time, I had also returned to work and Daniel was slowly coming off being breast-fed and moving on to formula and food. Eventually, when Daniel was nine months old I stopped breastfeeding altogether as it turned out I was already catering for two with Rebecca on the way.

Daniel didn't take to solids very well. He gagged, refused to eat, and was generally quite fussy. Continuous tummy aches and explosive nappies did not help matters. Having recently started nursery, we suspected tummy bugs were the cause and indeed for at least some of the time we were right. Daniel kindly shared them with us.

Over a period of time, things gradually improved and he managed to eat a varied if somewhat wet diet, until a further tummy bug seemed to destroy all sense of normality at mealtimes.

In December 2007, just after moving house, the compulsory Christmas tummy bug hit the family. At the time a family of four, we all got this sickness bug. Although only a twenty-four-hour thing, Daniel stopped eating. Eventually, he managed some toast, and for months afterwards it seemed all he would eat was toast.

Now, this is where things get interesting... no really! Until you take someone who is completely reliant on limited food sources for their intake, you really do not take into consideration the effects it can have. For those months, Daniel was eating little more than toast with the occasional maize snacks and drinking milk. There is a diet associated with autism known as the GFCF diet. This is gluten and casein free. Gluten can be found in flour and therefore in most types of bread and casein is a product found in dairy foods, of which milk is one. The idea is that GFCF (gluten free casein free) eliminates both gluten and casein from the diet, thereby reducing some of the challenging behaviours associated with autism.

Here is the science. The gluten and casein found in foods are addictive. In effect, Daniel had found himself addicted and as such craved only foods containing gluten and casein. With toast and milk on the menu, this addiction was being fed. The research suggests that the relationship between the stomach and brain is affected. The body does not process foods typically and the peptides produced from these food sources interact with the brain resulting in an opiate-like affect.

This is how it translated in Daniel:

Constantly raiding for food – Always gluten based, biscuits and bread!

Milk, Milk Milk! – At the time, we celebrated that Daniel drank his milk well. Actually it was a no-no!

Wide awake for most of the night – This was accompanied by what appeared to be extreme tummy cramps. We would find Daniel doubled up in pain and would sit massaging his belly for hours as the cramps eased off. We found that he often went from being highly distressed for a period of time followed by intermittent spells. The only thing I can liken it to was labour contractions in reverse. It was almost like his whole body was taken over by pain to start with followed by contractions that slowly got longer and longer apart, before he drifted off to sleep. At this stage, it was very much like he wanted to sleep but he simply couldn't. However, some days it seemed he had just had about enough sleep to get by and was then full of beans and ready to go... at 3am.

Hysterical Laughter – Yeast from the large quantities of bread caused a yeast overgrowth. This causes a reaction that disturbs the body from sleep and again changes behaviours with side effects such as hyperactivity and hysteria.

Awful nappies – Let's talk poop! Yes, this was and still is a topic of much discussion in our household. Daniel delivers some horrendous nappies.

> Boeing has this week been seeking FAA certification for a fix to their recent 787 battery problems. The solution involves an indestructible, fireproof, airtight box in which to locate the batteries. I believe the box design also includes a vent to the outside atmosphere in the event of the release of spewing electrolytes and/or noxious fumes, so they cannot enter the cabin. I think Boeing should consider a spin-off application for this box – with just a little bit of additional strengthening, I'd say this could be the ideal container to dispose of some of Daniel's (or indeed any child's) nappies. If it's ok, I'll email you our details, Mr. Boeing...

Eczema – The eczema continued and we removed all perfumed products and all synthetic fabrics. We used special washing powders and sensitive bathing products. We tried all the eczema solutions under the sun.

Zoned out – Actually like Daniel had been let loose on recreational drugs.

I recall sitting in a paediatric appointment re-coiling as I had to reel off Daniel's daily diet. The best piece of advice to come from that was not to worry about it as the tall, muscular and physically fit boy was the biggest indication that the diet, however limited or up and down, wasn't having a negative impact on his growth. Yet, food and drink is critical to survival and unless you have lived with someone who is on a limited diet by choice or medical need, you cannot really comprehend what it is like when someone simply refuses to eat something or swings the other way and eats to obsession and the repercussions it can have.

We eventually visited a nutritionist purely because we were concerned Daniel's diet was not nutritionally balanced. We hadn't even considered that the above issues were related. This is where we learnt that Daniel was likely to be at least intolerant of gluten or dairy and was also suffering from a yeast overgrowth, contributing to both his eczema and also an earlier bout of cradle cap that was incorrectly treated as impetigo.

So putting a child onto a gluten free and casein free diet is tough, really tough, but adding yeast into the mix is hell! You can get replacement milks but replacement bread, lacking milk, wheat flour and yeast, is quite a challenge. It looks like bread, yes! BUT finding something that tastes like bread and feels like bread, well that is really hard. It was possible to buy fairly basic small white gluten-free loaves, which were of limited appeal to Daniel. We then found it was possible to buy gluten- and dairy-free bread mixes... and we bought a bread maker. Okay, hands up – who has a bread maker in the kitchen? On a high shelf? That item under a dust cover (covered in dust)? Ours was humming on a nearly daily basis – possibly the most used bread maker in existence! But the bread costs maybe five or six times the price of your standard white Mother's Pride loaf at the supermarket. And it takes hours to prepare, mix, bake, wash up, slice... And finally, Daniel was eating around four or five slices a time – so the loaves were not lasting long. We think it made a difference for a while but as with a lot of food types, things go out of favour as quickly as they came in.

Add into the equation a little boy with very particular tastes and you almost need Willy Wonka to 'magic' up something. We haven't even started on the special beaker and plate. Yes, not only is Daniel fussy about what he eats, he is also particular about what he eats (and drinks) from and this alone can have him refusing to touch what is served up.

Goodbye Sleep

Part 2

However, the sleep issues didn't go away.

We managed to get into a pattern where one of us would sit with Daniel and he would eventually go to sleep. Whilst he was no longer experiencing the tummy aches in quite the same way, he had forgotten how to get himself off to sleep.

We went through sleep clinics, calming music, bedtime stories, a bath just before bed, no playing before sleep time. He just couldn't do it. Eventually, the paediatrician prescribed melatonin and for a while this was a godsend.

Melatonin is a naturally occurring hormone found in animals, plants, fungi and bacteria. It controls the natural night-day cycle and it was felt Daniel might not be producing enough of his to regulate this. Whilst no synthetic medication is entirely free of side effects, melatonin is deemed to be very safe.

To start with, Daniel would drift off to sleep within twenty minutes and sleep solidly through the night. However, we noticed that after a few months, whilst he was able to go to sleep, he wasn't staying asleep. Gradually it got worse and worse, to the point that he would be awake again before we had even gone up to bed.

The night waking wasn't just Daniel being awake and happily entertaining himself in his room. He became very distressed, waking up his younger sister next door and generally not safe to be left alone. He had a stair gate on his bedroom door but he would stand at it crying. And so, the night-time ritual started again. Any time between 11pm and 5pm we would find ourselves at the end of Daniel's bed for one, two, three hours or all night. There seemed to be no quick fix.

By this point, we were on our knees. Sympathy was in short supply as Daniel by this point (age 4) was still very much a little person and as such fellow parents jovially laughed off our gripes about the lack of sleep. Yet, the impact was immense because hours upon hours of a child in distress become wearing very quickly and you feel that no-one understands. We had another child; we KNEW what typical sleep deprivation was like and this wasn't it. There was no funny side of the story.

When is Enough Enough?

The reserves are low and the stakes high. So far, all else has failed. Yet, we didn't anticipate our son becoming a science experiment.

We all want to do whatever we can to help family or friends suffering from a disability or illness, whatever form that may take... Or do we?

Think of this... When we hear about a tragic accident on the news, let's say a train crash, in the aftermath we often hear, following the investigation, about deficiencies or errors, cost-cutting, mistakes made. People step forward and quite rightly state how appalled they are, and that all available safety measures should be put in place. "You can't put a price on safety, you can't put a price on human life" is a statement often quoted. If a system is available that could have saved lives, why on earth should it not have been employed? Surely this was an unforgivable omission?

Now, imagine this scenario... A brand new rail network is constructed, to run in parallel with the existing system, which remains. The new railway is state-of-the-art. No expense is spared. Every safety system imaginable has been employed and incorporated. Passengers are guaranteed a safe journey – virtually cosseted in cotton wool aboard an indestructible train. On launch day of the new network, the prices are announced. A round trip ticket to London costs £500. The old network, which still runs precisely as it does today, has a ticket for £20. I wonder which ticket the majority would buy?? I know what I would... I'd roll the dice and save myself £480.

So yes, isn't this saying that you *can* put a price on safety, in other words...?

Now returning to matter of disability within the family. When your own child suffers from a severe disability – in our case, autism, yes we wanted to do *anything* we could to help alleviate the distress, the pain, anxiety, the struggle to comprehend the world that our son faced on a daily basis. But when do you reach the point where "price IS an object", or in other words, enough is enough?

Supposing the effort to help your child takes up so much time and energy that you have to abandon your own hobbies, your own free time, your own social calendar and interests? Yet there is no guarantee that the effort will ultimately bear fruit and make any noticeable difference? How far do you go?

Supposing the effort to help your child costs so much money that you have to forget about a new car, a new television, a holiday or break of any kind, for you *or* your other children? How about if the expense is so much that you actually might risk facing financial ruination, debt, bankruptcy, the risk of even losing your home? Yet still there is no guarantee that the injection of money will ultimately bear fruit and make any noticeable difference? Do you throw every penny you've got and every one you can borrow into the fray?

Anyone who has seen the film "Lorenzo's Oil" will be aware of the sacrifices made by the parents for their son. How, when the doctors revealed there was no treatment or cure for their son's condition, they decided to dedicate their whole lives, their whole being, into educating themselves to whatever level was required, and ultimately develop a treatment themselves. It's a highly inspirational film and one I would recommend anyone to watch. But surely not realistic for every family?

When Daniel's diagnosis was announced, and later, when the severity of his autism and significant learning delays gradually became apparent, we did set out to try to fight "with everything we had" in our arsenal. We subscribed to newsletters and magazines, joined parents' groups, joined the National Autistic Society, scoured the internet to educate ourselves about the latest research and treatments, went out and bought recommended books on the subject. We tried nutritional therapy, we tried behavioural therapy, and we even flew to Manchester to attend an autism conference all about biomedical interventions. I'm satisfied that we exhausted as many options as we could to fight the diagnosis and help our son.

But there is a toll...

Let's take something simple – bread – as the first example. We had to bulk buy the special Gluten/Casein/Yeast free bread mix that Daniel consumed. Then we had to ensure we had a continuous supply, which could see us baking bread in the early hours whilst trying to entertain Daniel who was not only wide awake at 3am but very unhappy and hungry as well.

The bread is one of the more "high profile", or familiar, elements of something called nutritional therapy... which in itself is also a big part of what is termed biomedical intervention. Now we're getting somewhere... Biomedical intervention is a blanket term for the type of treatment that a "DAN" doctor (or practitioner) would prescribe. DAN stands for "Defeat Autism Now", and is based around the principle that the brain and the gut (i.e. what you eat, or what you put into your body and digest, in simple terms) are intrinsically linked. Put simply, the brain needs feeding the right combination of nutrients to function correctly, and hence problems with the functioning of the gut mean that some of those are not getting through (whilst other undesirable things *are* getting through). Sorting out the problems with digestion will ensure the brain is fed the correct stuff, and the "symptoms" of autism will be reduced.

So we contacted our nearest DAN practitioner, who agreed to meet us with Daniel, discuss his behaviour and diagnosis, and formulate a plan of action. I had read a lot online about the successes of DAN bio-medical interventions. You can find case studies on children, and testimonials from delighted parents. "Oh, Fred had this severe behaviour, David had never been able to speak, Billy had never coped with this and that... but since we pursued biomedical intervention, these problems have all amazingly improved or even disappeared." Sounds too good to be true?

Following our meeting and discussion with the DAN practitioner, a plan was recommended for Daniel which involved the prescription of a quite incredible (to me, at least) multitude of nutritional supplements. I'm not kidding – a vast series of tablets, capsules, vitamins and liquids, many of which I had never heard of, were all prescribed simultaneously. Some of these represented "super-doses" well in excess of the standard recommended daily intake for a healthy adult. When everything was totted up in price, we were looking at many hundreds of pounds per month expenditure to follow this recommended course of action, far more than we could realistically afford.

Various problems became clear to me at this point:

Firstly, how do you get a severely autistic child to take, chew, or swallow, voluntarily, such a vast daily set of supplements? The answer... You don't. Our practitioner was however clear that they needed to be administered "by any means". Capsules would need to be opened up and the powdered contents within mixed with something more palatable, such as a spoon of maple syrup. Tablets would need to be crushed with pestle and mortar (or in our case, the back of a teaspoon) and also mixed with the syrup. To administer the resultant concoction of chemicals, I would have to lie Daniel on the floor, sit astride him, with my knees across both arms preventing their movement. I would then hold his nose with one hand, forcing him to open his mouth, such that I could stick a syringe of the stuff into this throat and squirt everything in. Wow, does this not appear to border on cruelty? I'll let you make your own mind up about that!

There are only so many imaginative ways you can administer medication and Daniel, similar to the cat when due for worming, knows exactly when his food has been tampered with.

Secondly, we really couldn't afford the multitude of supplements initially recommended for Daniel. I asked the DAN practitioner to pare down the prescription to a subset he felt would represent the "higher priority" supplements. He was very resistant to this, I have to say, telling me "it really needs to be *all* of them ideally", although we did get him, somewhat reluctantly, to reduce the list.

Thirdly, how on *earth* do you ever hope to know which supplement is working and which is doing nothing (or even, which is making things *worse*) if so many are prescribed simultaneously? At the time I was an engineer, and also studied in the sciences at sixth form. As anyone will know, for a scientific experiment to be successful, if one is to assess the effects of changing various things, you must *only* change one at a time to make any sense of the results. There are no clear conclusions if you apply everything at once. It seemed to me that if, out of ten supplements, nine were found to have no effect, and one did, you could save a whole load of time and effort (and money) by eliminating the nine duds.

In my view, we did "the best of a bad job" in this instance. Our cupboard looked like the back room of the local pharmacy for a while with the many pots, jars and bottles stacked up. I did my best to minimise distress for Daniel by giving him the syringe load in the mouth as swiftly and painlessly as it was physically possible to do – but, let's be clear, the poor lad *did not like it.* We had gagging, tears, tantrums, spitting out... It's not a time in our battle that I feel particularly proud of. And, despite all the effort, did it make the huge difference we were hoping for? Well actually... No. Did it make any difference whatsoever? Well actually... probably not, or not noticeably anyway. We saw no "miracle improvement" in our son for our efforts. And we put him through a whole lot of discomfort and upset and drained hundreds if not thousands of pounds of our limited, hard earned cash, in the process.

As I look back, I wonder now... Was it actually better that we saw no discernible improvement from our efforts? Because, it's tough on us, tough on Daniel, and tough on the bank balance to maintain for a protracted period. Suppose we thought we had seen a *small* improvement? It's possible we would have persisted with the tablets, the potions, the syringes, the gagging, the tantrums and everything else for far longer than we did. I'm also aware there are many other forms of treatment over and above what we tried. Some people inject vitamin doses into their child's backside on a regular basis to be sure they get into the body. Some try sealing their little child into oxygen chambers for hours on end... Others swear that electro-magnetic radiation is a contributing culprit, and relocate their family to a locale as isolated from civilisation as possible, no mobile phones, WiFi, Bluetooth, etc. There are solid scientific rationales behind many if not all of these – we're not talking crackpot theories in most cases.

But when is enough enough? We tried, we did our best – we really did – but for us, it didn't lead to a miraculous or hoped-for improvement. And as I write this, we are not haemorrhaging money or upsetting our child on a daily basis. And I feel we – our whole family – are in a happier position as a consequence.

Good luck to anyone else who follows the path of biomedical intervention for their child. All I would say is, be mindful of the cost... and be prepared to take a step back and re-assess what you hope to get out of this, should you not see a miracle unfolding...

ABA to Learn Your ABCs, Amongst Other Things

ABA is a series of techniques and principles used to bring positive change in behaviour and as a tool to enhance development.

Applied Behavioural Analysis = ABA

We attempted ABA Therapy around the time Daniel was four and initially saw an increase in his attention span, eye contact and communication using PECS.

ABA is commonly discussed in the autism world, and opinion is split as to whether it is the best method of intervention in overcoming autistic traits.

So what is ABA?

ABA is a series of techniques and principles used to bring positive change in behaviour and as a tool to enhance development. The main strategy is that the taught person is rewarded with positive reinforcement when they complete a task or act in an appropriate way. As such the individual is more likely to repeat, advance or act appropriately because it is rewarded positively. Whilst the positives are recognised, negative behaviours are completely ignored. This is because some negative behaviours serve as a means of getting desired attention. The individual has to learn that this is not the way to get attention. The word 'NO' is all but banned.

A very simple exercise carried out with Daniel recently. Daniel had to sit appropriately and choose between two balloons. To break this down, Daniel had to sit down and listen to the instruction where he was being asked to choose something:

The motivator was the balloons as he loves them to be blown up and then let down.

The deviation from this was that Daniel may have not been sitting for the duration and may not have been fully focused on the activity, just assuming that a balloon would be blown up for him. By repetition, Daniel learnt that the balloon wouldn't be presented unless he was sitting and watching and wouldn't be blown up unless he chose one. By the end of the session, Daniel was almost requesting an appropriate Makaton sign to accompany his request for the balloon, one stage further. A long-term aim might be to 'say' balloon by choosing an appropriate picture card (PECS), sign language or even speech.

PECS, or Picture Exchange Communication System, was first introduced to us as a method of communication delivered initially in an ABA session. PECS is the exchange of a picture representing the wanted object or service. Daniel completed the first stage of PECS, which is Phase 1. This means he learnt that handing over the appropriate card led to him receiving the reward as indicated in the picture. He soon moved onto Phase 2, which is distance. This means he had to travel with the card to the person offering the reward, who may have been situated out of sight or in another room. This is in recognition that the person or object may not be in sight but is still available with the right request. Phase 3 is discrimination and whilst Daniel has had some success with choosing between two items or more items, he doesn't retain this skill and will sometimes hand over any card in the hope that he will get what he wants. The end aim is to build up to whole sentences using the card system. PECS is universally used and does not have to go hand in hand with an ABA programme.

So, this all sounds very positive. Why would anyone object to this method of intervention? Well, to achieve the best results you have to work intensively and consistently. For us, once the intensity of ABA was left behind, Daniel regressed back to his old ways very quickly. It is also doesn't solve every issue. Living with autism presents new challenges and once you have overcome one, you often find yourself with two or three more to replace it.

The 'full-on' approach has been criticised for producing children who are robot-like, and so reliant on the ABA method that they struggle more with spontaneity than ever. The process is regimented and some say that it does not allow a child to be, well, a child. Equally, a lot of individuals on the spectrum thrive on routine and really struggle when their timetable is thrown off track. Whilst ABA can be very re-petitive and favour routine, life isn't like that and some would say that ABA makes it more regimented, not less. Attempting to incorporate ABA into your daily routine can also be challenging and it is tiring, both to deliver and reciprocate.

From my experience with ABA, I would say that the benefits out-weigh the negative aspects. However, we were never able to do a full time programme due to financial and time constraints. In theory, the principles can be delivered to anyone, not just those with additional needs. That said, as for any parent, ignoring what are deemed as bad behaviours can be a real challenge and losing the use of the word 'NO', well, that is the hardest thing of all.

Ultimately ABA offers support in overcoming challenges that present with autism BUT it isn't a cure.

A Bum Smear

I've stood back and tried the 'wide angle' view following an episode of smearing – and I've yet to identify a stunning image.

Whilst flicking through a copy of the Oxford English dictionary earlier, I was able to look up the definition of a *"bum steer"*, described as *"A piece of false information or unhelpful guidance"*. However, when glancing just a few lines further up the page, I found myself unable to locate an equivalent entry for the term *"bum smear"*.

Yet this term could, sadly, be an ideal term to describe an activity widely experienced by parents of children (or indeed, adults) at the more severe end of the autistic spectrum. For anyone not clear what I am talking about, here is the definition in plain (and painful) English – *the smearing of one's own poo, liberally about the immediate surroundings. Can include smearing onto your own body including the face and in the hair, etc...*

Yes, it's graphic. It's smelly, and by that I mean *it really reeks*. It's the most incredibly disgusting mess you've ever seen. I wonder how many reading this in the UK will remember those old BBC children's art shows, usually featuring Tony Hart (think "Vision On" if you're old enough, then later "Take Hart" and "Hart Beat"). Sometimes Tony Hart would produce an enormous mural by liberally splashing and smearing multi-coloured paint onto a large, blank wall or floor, either with hands or a variety of brushes or sponges. The resultant image would often appear to be a random 'mess' when viewed close up, only revealed to be a stunning image of a yacht at sea, or some other masterful image when viewed through a more distant wide-angle camera shot.

I've stood back and tried the 'wide angle' view following an episode of smearing – and I've yet to identify a stunning image. From this I can only conclude that perhaps Daniel is more into Modern Art. And it's usually only in shades of brown...

Whilst it's possible, with hindsight and given the healing effect that the passage of time provides, to look back on these incidents with a certain measure of humour – at the time they are exceptionally distressing and upsetting to deal with. And if there is only one parent or carer present – the logistics of dealing with the aftermath of a smearing incident are nigh-on impossible. How do you look after a severely autistic child, get them cleaned up and bathed, but also get the surrounding environment cleaned up as well? How do you even get them from their current location to the bathroom without causing peripheral damage (i.e. mess) to the floor and/or walls that must be traversed in the journey, then keep them static whilst filling the bath and removing soiled clothing? Then keep them clean and safe whilst scrubbing carpets, walls and furniture (without them touching anything in between...). Perhaps there's a new game here for contestants to figure out if they ever re-launch "The Crystal Maze"...

With Daniel, the 'peak' of smearing activities probably occurred around the age of four or five – certainly old enough to be out of Babygros, and now in normal trousers, t-shirts, pyjamas – and with enough motor skill now developed to easily 'insert hands' inside a recently soiled nappy.

It's fairly obvious to see that the best solution to all of this had to be to take preventative measures – stop the smearing in the first place, at all costs! There are two ways to do this, either (i) watch Daniel every second of the day and night, or (ii) find some suitable clothing for him to wear during periods when not being monitored, that prevents any easy access to the 'nappy area'. This basically means bigger-sized Babygros, dungarees, 'romper suits', leotards or any other type of 'all-in-one' outfit that covers the bottom area.

Go into any branch of Primark, M&S or any of the big supermarket chains these days, and you are spoilt for choice with a huge range of 'onesies' from small child size right up to strapping six-feet-plus adult, in a huge number of colours and themes from super-heroes to fairies. Hard to believe, then, that back in around 2008 all of these were virtually unheard of! You simply could not find anything remotely suitable on the British High Street. We searched high and low to find any type of all-in-one clothing for Daniel, scouring the internet for options. At that point, we would in all likelihood have shipped in some clothing from the Fiji Islands if they had something appropriate on sale. At one point I remember we bought a pair of standard pyjamas, and a set of sew-on press-studs to try to manufacture our own set of non-removable pyjamas – not a success sadly, for the main reason that the 'popper resistance strength' (is there an actual technical term for this?) was too weak, and the things would just detach at the slightest prompting.

Eventually we found something suitable called the "little-keeper sleeper" suit, which we paid to ship in from the USA – basically an all-in-one suit accessed via a zip on the back (held shut with two poppers, and virtually impossible for a child to undo), and finally were able to leave the room at night without fear of an impromptu 'brown party' in our son's adjacent bedroom.

Since then, for the most part we have, via an array of different garments ranging from Lycra swimsuits (one was bright pink – sorry Daniel!) to leotards and onesies, managed to steer clear of the smear... That's not to say we don't have the occasional accidents, nappy containment failures, and near-miss smearing episodes.

Pah – these are nothing to an experienced smearer-clearer...
...although
...can I take that back? It's still very, very grim.

Adding to a Family with an Existing Child with Autism

They say that it is harder going from no children to one. When contemplating our third, it was our first child who was the deciding factor.

One of the most controversial questions we face is why we decided to have a third child. In particular, making this decision knowing that the risk of autism was increased and aware of the challenges Daniel was already experiencing by then.

Well firstly, autism is a spectrum of conditions and each individual is affected differently. It is a personal choice whether to extend a family or not and the most important question we had to ask ourselves is whether we could cope with three children, let alone another on this spectrum.

For me personally, if I could change one thing for my son it would be that the periods of distress he experiences could cease. More than anything else I want him to be happy, healthy and content, and if the diagnosis of autism remained but he had all of those things, so be it. Life with a child with autism isn't all doom and gloom. Daniel has some lovely characteristics that his siblings lack. He doesn't show jealousy and generally will share nicely. He is more likely to listen and follow instruction and he gives the most satisfying giggle if tickled. I suspect Daniel is more aware of the mischief behind some of his actions than we give credit for but as a rule he doesn't manipulate or provoke.

It is also fair to point out that although Daniel had already started to experience very distressing behaviour whilst I was pregnant with Sophie, we still didn't realise the severity of his autism. Only the passage of time with no real development in social skill, extended periods of sleep deprivation, a maturing Daniel and increased challenging behaviour has really allowed that to sink in.

Despite all this, the decision to have little Sophie, a very much-wanted little girl, was not easy. We had a beautiful boy and girl already. It was greedy to want another having been blessed with two... well yes, maybe, but there were other factors.

Ultimately the decision was ours to make, that and Mother Nature's. I personally wouldn't judge someone who decided not to have children, who couldn't have children, had settled for one child, two children, whatever number.

I have always wanted a big family. For much of my childhood I was an only child, although I do now have a beautiful younger sister. I'd always envisaged a sibling to share life's dramas with to be a wonderful thing, be it for a game, a snuggle, sibling squabbles, the happy times and the sad. That isn't to say being an only child is any less happy but in my mind a sibling would have been great.

We had a beautiful boy and a beautiful girl but one of those individuals would need lifetime support. Who was going to do that when we were no longer able to? This was and remains a scary prospect for us and although we know that Daniel has years to progress and flourish, realistically he will need lifelong support.

It would be unfair to expect Daniel's siblings to look after him when they will have lives, possibly families of their own. Despite this, I guess we hope by that stage that a genuine bond will ensure that both Rebecca and Sophie remain close to their brother and that they have each other for support if they do decide to be involved in his life decisions. Prior to Sophie's arrival, Rebecca did have a big brother but sadly the relationship isn't that of typical siblings. Time will tell whether that will change as both grow up. For Daniel, having siblings who he is familiar with and able to experience a typical childhood alongside can only be positive.

Rebecca was already born when Daniel was diagnosed. At three years of age, she exhibited no signs of being on the spectrum. This would have given us some confidence that for every chance we would have a child on the spectrum, there was a chance that we would not and if we did, we already had some insight.

In those early years of diagnosis we read EVERYTHING we could get our hands on and investigated Speech and Language based therapies, nutritional therapies, and behavioural approaches, and tried to educate ourselves as best we could. The thing is, autism remains a learning curve, and I don't think anyone can truly say they fully understand the condition or how to manage it.

There are sacrifices though on both sides. Having three children isn't easy and the house is often chaotic. This goes against the idyllic conditions for Daniel, one-to-one in a calm routine driven environment – hah – try explaining that to a strong-minded blue-eyed girl or an articulate sensitive young lady. There is the constant battle for attention and trying to ensure all their needs are met, ferrying to relevant schools and playgroups, attending appointments and the like. There are financial implications from having multiple childcare  costs and also the increased cost of specialist services for Daniel. Both the girls have had to witness some very distressing behaviour from their brother, periods of prolonged crying and sleepless nights where he has kept them awake... again upset. We try to protect them as much as we can but all we can hope for is that they are educated to understand why these spells occur and learn from it within their tolerance of others. Daniel does have a couple of nights away from home so that the girls get to do something with Mummy and Daddy that Daniel might not have tolerated.

We also completely respect that some parents decide not to have any more children once they have one diagnosed on the spectrum. All their efforts may be spent trying to ensure that their child is given as much opportunity as possible and whether they would have originally considered having more, it is no longer part of the equation. We do our best by Daniel but ultimately we have two other children to look after.

All three of our children are a blessing but I would be the first to admit that the path we chose was possibly not the easiest one and we have made mistakes along the way for sure. Yet I stand by the decision to have a third as being the best we could have made for us. All three share the same cheeky laugh and twinkle in their eye. They all bring something different to our lives and each other's.

Don't Call Me Danny

Sometimes something as simple as your name, matters.

Our little boy knows his name – it's Daniel. However, in the early days it was apparent something was awry when early indications were that he didn't. Initial tests were carried out to ensure Daniel could hear. That first test led to more, raised by the concern that the problem wasn't so much hearing but issues with social interaction.

Daniel attended a mainstream nursery and could pick out his name card with prompting. It may be that he recognised the colour or the letter sequence but still, he wouldn't necessarily respond if you called his name. The hearing tests previously mentioned were clear and there was no reason to believe that Daniel had anything other than good hearing. In hindsight we know that he can actually hear extremely well and we have to think very carefully before using the microwave, vacuum cleaner or lawn mower.

Daniel will, once he has processed the words, usually respond if we keep a request simple but we have to use Daniel. Danny, Dan, cheeky, smelly and any other affectionate name we call him simply does not register. The only deviation to this was when Sophie started to crawl and get herself into mischief. Daniel would respond to her being told "Sophie, no" by becoming upset himself. I can only assume that he registers the two syllables' similarity.

Daniel has always had good receptive language and can understand simple instructions: "Daniel, go upstairs", "Daniel, school bus", "Daniel, dinner". This is good and one half of the battle against the loss of communication skills, but there are limitations.

Daniel doesn't understand questions such as "why do you...?", "where is...?", or "what are you doing?" He will come if we say "Daniel, shoes," but as he cannot put his shoes on independently, and doesn't respond to "go get your shoes".

So Daniel will always be "Daniel". It sounds simple enough doesn't it? Yet, when we hear Danny, Dan, young man, and we find ourselves correcting to 'Daniel' we cannot help but feel obtuse but it does MATTER, it isn't a preference, it is a necessity to clear communication. We have to make it easy for Daniel to understand what we expect of him because the real battle is in getting him to tell us what he expects of us.

Fear and Bath-Time

What is the fear as it obviously isn't water alone?

As a new parent, bathing a baby Daniel was a time of joy and laughter, the coos and splashes. I guess it was something I took for granted.

So, I was faced with a fairly cheerful Daniel casually skipping up the stairs to bed, when he realised, it's BATH NIGHT. Then the mood changed...

Daniel loves water, water pistols, hosepipe, watering cans, swimming, walking in the rain but currently baths and showers... not at all. It does vary though and sometimes he will quite happily play in the bath. On occasion, last year, he was even able to have five minutes play in the bath with us observing from just outside the room. That was until he discovered that he could tip a whole litre of water onto the floor with his hair jug. We do not tend to face him with the shower option as he really doesn't like it and attempts have led to him struggling to settle thereafter. Bath-time does not occur every night for this very reason because it is all too traumatic.

The fear seemed to increase. There is more to it than simply not liking having his hair washed, and it was accompanied by increased anxiety surrounding toilet visits and having his face wiped in case they were followed by a bath. At the same time we appreciated that at some point he was going to need more than wet wipes to keep his hygiene in check.

So having persuaded Daniel to go into the bath-room, his fears are confirmed and in front of him stands a bath full of bubbles. On occasion, he will giggle and put the taps on or play with the bubbles but last night he was positive that there was no way he was going in that bath. Usually after a little coaxing, we can get him to step in the bath as he clings on to us for dear life. Last night, he was not having it. I tried to guide him to the bath; he went and sat down on the toilet. I managed to get him to stand up again and then he ran out of the bathroom. Having guided him back in, I tried to lift him up. A big NO on two accounts. On doing so, he immediately dropped to the ground and proceeded to wriggle so that I couldn't hold him in any fashion. This is where the benefit of his trampoline built muscle comes into play; oh boy is he strong and when he drops on you, your body knows about it. Well my back did that day...

By this time, Daniel is notably frightened and his legs are shaking but I know he needs to have some kind of wash down. He will reach for his pyjamas in the hope that you will see sense and dress him. Yet, there is food in his hair and he needs a soaking and he really isn't going to school in the morning with tomato ketchup remains.

Finally, realising that I am not going to give in, Daniel steps into the bath. This isn't, however, without a vice-like grip on both my hands or to the edge of the bath. So, we now have Daniel in the bath and sitting down but I am unable to do anything to wash him because every time I try to release a hand, he'll grab me elsewhere. Once we are both covered in bubbles, some empty bottles he likes to play with distract him. Then Mummy attacks by pouring water onto his hair and you'd think I was torturing him. Maybe in his mind I was but in winter this is how it goes.

In summer, things are a little easier. Daniel doesn't get out of bath-time but the hose in the garden, water pistols etc. and the opportunity to get into a cool bath seem to make bath-time more favourable in the warmer months. I have considered whether the bath needs to be cooler in the winter or whether the air temperature needs to be warmer. However, I really think it is just down to the fact that he desensitised because water features more regularly in his everyday life.

That said, Daniel is currently swimming at school and so is exposed to the routine of changing that bit more frequently. Maybe, it is just too much for him to cope with. All I know is that the 45cm height advantage I have on him brings nothing to trying to get him into the bath. It may be that we need to go down a sensory approach and introduce flashing lights and toys that make it more fun. Historically, though, said toys have been rejected until after the bath has finished, when he will happily play with them.

After probably less than three minutes in the bath, I tell Daniel it is time to get out. With this, he literally leaps out bringing half the bath water with him, straight into Mummy's arms. With the towel placed around him, the sense of relief is evident, and buried in the biggest bath towel, you may hear a little giggle as we towel dry his hair.

Somewhere out of the neighbouring bedroom, Rebecca comes into the bathroom and glances around at the flooded floor and bubbles up the wall tiles. "Has Daniel finished his bath?"

The bathroom has worse to come – two hyper girls sharing it with full range of bath toys, more bubbles and more water to be distributed outside the tub – but for Daniel, the ordeal is over. I often wonder in the years to come, whether it will be a 6ft man that I am trying to persuade that bath-time is fun.

When the Added
Extra Costs Money

In the end, everything comes down to money.

Any discussion on childcare has to look at the expense and affordability of it (whatever 'it' turns out to be), and therefore has to look at the ability to generate money, e.g. work! All three are interlinked – which makes this a bit of a monster of a topic to try to cover here!

I am usually wary of statistics – I often feel they can be 'skewed' or presented in such a 'selective' or misleading way as to reinforce pretty much any side of any argument. Tabloid newspapers are particularly good at this. So, having said all that, when thinking about what to write on the subject of childcare for Daniel, please excuse me for opening with some statistics myself!

"Autism is expensive. It costs, on average, three times as much money to raise a child with a serious disability than it does to raise a non-disabled one." (quote taken from the 'ambitious about autism' website)

So clearly if we are to be able to afford childcare for Daniel, it looks like we are going to pay 'above the odds' to find something appropriate for his needs (not that 'mainstream' childcare is cheap to start with!)

I feel it's high time for the next statistic...

"Unfortunately, autism also an issue that often affects your ability to earn money. Only 11% of parents with autistic children are able to work full-time, and 70% of parents say that they don't have enough support to be able to work as much as they need..."

But hang on – can we not assume that childcare is only really required for the purpose of enabling us to work... to pay for the childcare? Obviously this is a ridiculously simplistic argument and only a very small part of it... besides which, the income is needed to pay for a whole lot more than just childcare. But, as any parents with a severely autistic child will be only too aware, the *hardest job* is actually likely to be the looking after your child, NOT the 'office job', a child who requires round the clock care, who cannot speak or communicate, who is not toilet trained, who is frequently distressed, who lashes out at loved ones, who cries and screams all night long, seven nights a week, week in, week out... To stand a chance of remaining sane and coping for the long term, we as parents need respite care, a break from the relentless battle to care for and keep our child safe and healthy.

So childcare is actually needed for two purposes – in order to work, and for respite care. So we are not only facing having to pay considerably more for appropriate childcare, but also ideally we need it for twice the duration. It just gets worse!

Here's a final sobering quotation I've taken from an article in CNN Money that sums up the position many parents of autistic children – including us – are faced with:

"The burden on families affected by autism is enormous. Immediately parents are faced with bills that are not being covered so they turn to second mortgages or home equity lines of credit, then they turn to credit cards and other family members and at that point they are out of options."

The 'burden on families' referred to here is, of course, not just childcare, but the costs involved in ALL aspects of raising a child with special needs. So we have to include in that various behavioural or nutritional therapies, supplements, special furniture and adaptations to the home, special clothing, nappies, wipes and other toiletries. They all add significant costs – and some way has to be figured out to pay for them!

To pay for them, we have to work. And to work we must have childcare.

Looking back to our decisions concerning childcare for Daniel, these went through numerous permutations as we struggled to deal with his diagnosis, and the various logistics needed as we both struggled to work and earn sufficient income to support our growing family.

As with most children, Daniel's unique needs and difficulties didn't arrive overnight, and during his pre-school years we mostly managed to make use of mainstream childcare – Daniel attended a "Peter

Bunny" nursery not far from our workplace(s) when still a baby, then moved to the "First Steps" nursery closer to home as a toddler. It was here, following Daniel's initial diagnosis of autism at age two, that the problems started to emerge, as Daniel entered his period of regression – failing to make progress in all areas while surrounded by his peers who continued to rapidly advance beyond his capabilities.

At home, the situation continued to deteriorate. Daniel, as well as losing the very few "babbled words" that had formed in his early vocabulary, started to become withdrawn, disinterested in interacting in any meaningful social way with family/friends or us. He made no progress with toilet training, and started suffering sleeping issues (or rather, lack of sleeping issues...) including what appeared to be regular severe tummy aches and constant crying and distress – often for most if not all of the night. Getting Daniel to eat was proving difficult, with his self-restricted diet reducing to pretty much solely toast for a time.

The situation for us, as parents, fast became absolutely horrendous. At times we were awake for night after night after night, endlessly trying to deal with our beautiful son's never-ending distress, cries, shrieks and pained wailing throughout the wee hours – this was occurring virtually EVERY night, for weeks and months. And, all the while, we both attempted to work a full time office job.

At one stage I recall days when I was so sleep deprived and exhausted, I would spend part of my lunch hour at work in my car – I would intentionally park in a far corner of the car park, such that I could sneak myself away for a few minutes' nap there. Oh the bliss for those few minutes of actual silence... peace and quiet, unheard of at any other time of day. One day I was so sleep deprived I inadvertently filled the car with unleaded fuel (the car took diesel), and virtually burst into tears when I realised. Other days I barely recalled driving into the office or to nursery at all, operating totally on 'autopilot', arriving with no memory of having performed the trip. Some days I became absolutely despairing of the situation – it appeared there was no future or anything to look forward to beyond dealing with the endless distress. How long would we be expected to stand it? How long could anyone reasonably stand this, without succumbing to depression or some kind of mental breakdown?

In the end, we decided that we urgently needed an injection of additional childcare. At this stage, cost seemed a distant, secondary concern when compared to the potential benefits to our sanity if nothing else! By this stage Daniel was still accessing mainstream childcare for a few short hours during weekdays at "First Steps" nursery, but we needed more help outside this time. After considering various options, we finally decided that our only realistic option was to employ a nanny.

When most people think of a 'nanny', they probably associate the term with the Royal Family, or at the very least the 'upper classes' or aristocracy. Well, either that or Mary Poppins flying in with her brolly! However, a nanny turned out to actually be the most realistic option for us... being basically a child-minder who works in your home rather than their own. No need to take Daniel somewhere unfamiliar, no concerns about him fitting in with other children, no need to worry he will act oddly or be distressed or violent amongst other children, no concerns about him breaking other people's possessions, no endless runs to drop off and pick up around work hours. The next decision we had to make was whether to go for a live-in or live-out nanny. Did we really want to invite a stranger to come and live with us in our own home? There are financial advantages to employing a live-in nanny – if you have a spare room, you are effectively paying for their accommodation, food, heating, electricity and water, so the regular salary you offer is appropriately reduced to account for this. But how do you choose someone – how do you know if they are honest, reliable, consistent, polite, trustworthy...?

Our families made their concerns about inviting an extra person to live with us known. However, the potential benefits – particularly given our fatigue and state of mind at the end – outweighed any negatives and after a relatively short search we took on our first nanny in November 2008, conveniently allocating the extra bedroom in our attic in our house for their accommodation.

Thankfully – it worked out well. Our instincts at the interview stage turned out to be spot on concerning the person we chose, and the help we so urgently required with Daniel to survive was suddenly there. As it turned out we also made a good friend. An important point to remember here is that having a live-in nanny did not suddenly mean we had 'round the clock' childcare on tap. A nanny is paid for the hours they work, and as with most jobs, the evenings and weekends were their own time – so we still had to care for the children during evenings, night-waking and weekends. But the psychological benefit of having that extra person around, and the ability to ask for occasional extra help at short notice, just made everything somehow that bit more manageable during those really difficult times.

...And so began a two-and-a-half-year period when we employed a nanny (actually, three) who lived with us and provided very urgently needed childcare. All three proved to be conscientious, friendly and reliable and a great help.

The financial burden, however, remains enormous. We may have acquired the help we need, but at what price? An incoming salary far outweighed by our outgoings, savings evaporating, credit cards racking up balances that we can't pay off. What do you do when placed in a 'no win' scenario?

You simply make it up as you go along. Troubles piled up for the future are not troubles now, after all. And financial concerns are but one of the many issues we are likely to face in the coming years.

Medication is All You (Don't) Need

When medicine is not a magic potion.

Daniel's decline always tends to be in summer. While the summer months allow for Daniel's favourite pastime, trampolining, there is a downside to the endless days outside of school. He struggles with heat (ha – England), wet weather (more likely), change in routine but also hay fever. As a child with eczema, sadly the two go hand in hand. You would think that to resolve this it would take a simple trip to the pharmacy. Actually no, as for reasons unexplained, just as Daniel isn't 'typical' – neither is his reaction to medication. Our boy is complex, autism is complex and so is biology! This is the boy who will bounce off walls if you give him a new-born dosage of syrup suspended analgesic.

There is a tendency in popular culture to treat the symptoms of an ailment, rather than get to the root of the cause. Sometimes, this leads to no further ill effects but every now and then you will read something that makes you stop and think. Occasionally, a rather annoying symptom isn't just us fighting the latest bug, that cough that just will not shift or having an off day, those headaches that occur frequently – but something more sinister lurking. That isn't to say that every time we are a bit off colour we should go into panic that we have some fearful disease BUT sometimes we do need to slow down and listen to what our bodies are telling us.

In a lot of ways, the treatments available for autism follow a similar path. In Daniel's first ten years, there have been three occasions where medication has been prescribed in response to the signs of distress, anxiety and psychotic behaviours. Now, this is really tricky because Daniel cannot tell us what is wrong so we can only go on his body language, physical examination and a lot of guesswork to actually establish what is going on.

The first occasion was back when Daniel was three years old. He had a very unsettled summer, very little sleep and became very aggressive, tearful and a hive of pent up energy. He was prescribed something to help him sleep. I forget the name now but it was basically a tranquiliser often given to people with severe phobias such as for flying to sedate them. Obviously it was prescribed in a small dose but oh boy, it had the opposite effect on Daniel and he was completely wired.

This behaviour in someone so small is incredibly stressful and frightening. It far surpasses the typical tantrum and trying to explain to those around you that you are frightened of a three-year-old is not really taken seriously. Yet, in these situations there are no boundaries to strength and a minor, however short they may be, is able to deliver a nasty smack or punch or kick. Besides the physical injury, the emotional fall out is immense. There is no logic or reasoning in an autism meltdown.

The second occasion was some two years later, in summer, and was just the same albeit with a very young Sophie in tow. We debated over contributing factors; Daddy was away for work, we had a relatively new baby, and it was summertime. This time Daniel was prescribed Equasym. Equasym is commonly prescribed for ADHD, a condition that sees the sufferer unable to concentrate, with short attention spans and high levels of energy, low danger awareness and often aggression. Daniel was experiencing a lot of these issues so although he wasn't thought to have ADHD, a trial was suggested to calm him down and hopefully regain some attention span so that we could then work with him to keep him calm.

We kept a diary to monitor progress and here is an excerpt:

Started Daniel on Ritalin (Equasym XL) today. He has been reasonably calm this week but was really hitting himself this morning. Daddy is poorly so he might be anxious about a change in routine. So within an hour of administering the medicine, he hit Sophie twice... hard. He seldom goes for her and from first impressions his aggression is up.

Daniel would develop a dullness to his eyes not long after taking his morning medication and with it his agitation would escalate. It was almost like he was not sedated enough to be calm but aware that things weren't right either. By late afternoon he would return to a more reasonable mood only to see the return of the distress and anger by bedtime, shortly after the second dose. When it became apparent that the Equasym wasn't working we were referred for sleep support, routines put in place for holiday time, and if nothing else, someone else seeing what we were coping with really helped. Eventually we made the decision to discontinue with the Equasym and things gradually got better over a period of months.

In hindsight I think that the medication actually elevated the behaviours as opposed to blotting them out. Sometimes you have to weigh up what is worse, the behaviours or the medication that is meant to be alleviating them.

Hot Weather? No Sweat...

The perspiration left a glint across his brow... or indeed, it didn't but instead his temperature rose like a pressure cooker.

Well here we are firmly entrenched in our first round of traditional, British 'stifling hot with no air or relief' summer (as opposed to traditional 'sodden, torrential' British summer, or the recent traditional 'unusually cold for this time of year with gale force winds' summer) and our annual heat-related difficulties with Daniel have reared their ugly head once again.

What? You thought the title "No Sweat" suggested that Daniel breezes through heat waves with no problem? No... in this instance I *literally* mean "No Sweat". As in Daniel does not appear to sweat. Daniel's genetic make-up represents the things of nightmares for antiperspirant manufacturers such as Lynx and Sure (although possibly their salvation would lie within the adjacent deodorant department, as Daniel is certainly not odour-free).

There is an episode of the 70s TV show "The Six Million Dollar Man" where a bad guy genius scientist creates a perfect robot replica of OSI boss and Steve Austin's pal Oscar Goldman (this is showing my age now). In the final scene, Austin is faced with both Oscars – real and robot –and has to decide which to take out. Both continue to plead that they are the *real* Oscar. At this point, Steve cleverly makes use of his bionic super-vision (those familiar with the show will now be re-creating the bionic "boop boop beep beep beep" sound that accompanied use of this vision). He sees that one Oscar is sweating profusely but the other remains completely dry, and is able to, after an exciting bionic tussle, despatch the robot Oscar via a head-removing blow from a long metal scaffold/pole.

So, what I'm saying is this – faced with the real Daniel and replica robot Daniel, Austin would have trouble... real trouble... since neither sweat. As an aside, to further complicate and confuse matters, both the robot *and* real Daniel would also possess bionic strength. (We witness this whenever attempting to cut Daniel's hair, but there's a story for another day!)

Back to the topic in hand, and to sum up – during very hot weather, Daniel gets upset. <u>Very</u> upset. And often, very frequently. This is a pattern that we have observed on an annual basis for several years now. This year, until a week or two ago, appeared to have "skipped" summer and landed right in mid-autumn. We'd had unusually low temperatures, frequent rain, and gale force winds... and Daniel had for the most part been happy. The hot weather arrived and he switched into full-on grump mode.

So one question we have asked ourselves is this – could Daniel's reluctance to sweat or effectively regulate his body temperature somehow be connected to this? It's one of many questions we will never know the answer to. But it does appear that Daniel's body does not respond to hot or cold in the traditional sense. Daniel will quite happily venture out and play on his favourite trampoline in the glacial conditions of an arctic winter. Coat? What coat? Don't really need socks on for ice, do we? This jumper is proving an inconvenience... I'll take it off... As parents, we run outside in rain, snow, hail and wind, grimacing against the sub-zero wind chill to pull a happily bouncing Daniel indoors. Does he care? No!!

This brings us to the heatwave conditions of the past week. It's fair to say Daniel is active. Even if he's not energetically leaping or jumping on the trampoline, he will be furiously chewing the safety netting – and that expends energy, right? And if he's not sweating, does that mean that his core body temperature is rising above what would normally be considered appropriate or safe? The rest of us become uncomfortably warm and start sweating buckets to cool down – so what happens with Daniel? If the body, including the brain, warms above the usual fairly tight range of human operating temperature, what effect could that have? My guess would be discomfort and distress, based on what we see with Daniel. These past few days Daniel has been upset, inconsolable at times, often for long periods and often without warning, and it always increases in frequency when the weather is hot.

And what can we do about it? Well, herein lies another substantial problem for us:

(i) Reduce clothing? 'No can do' – Daniel is prone to stripping and subsequent toileting, so has to wear some type of all-in-one clothing, especially at night.

(ii) Open windows? 'No can do' – Daniel has no "safety awareness" so an open window in his bedroom is an invitation for trouble. To further restrict things, neither of our girls will allow for an "open window" policy at night-time either. Apparently (according to three-year-old Sophie) this could lead to a "Sly" in her room. And before you ask why she could possibly dislike rugged actor Sylvester Stallone, let me just confirm this is a three-year-old, and a "Sly" could easily be confused with a small household airborne insect...

(iii) Air conditioning? 'No can do' – Daniel dislikes noise, particularly from household appliances such as vacuum cleaners, dishwashers or extractor fans. We do have a portable air conditioner, but you may as well invite a gang of Hell's Angels to rev up on the landing, and you still wouldn't hear them when the air conditioner switch is turned on.

This evening I tried a spray bottle of water, but it was immediately clear that was unpopular too.

So... I suspect we shall stick it out as usual, and wait for the cooler conditions. What a shame though, as it's lovely to have a period of warmth and sunshine!

A further comment, however, that we found interesting. When

Daniel's dislike of heat was raised on an Autism Support internet page, we found we were not alone in our findings. Many other parents responded with very similar tales of troubles during the hot weather. I wonder... I haven't checked, but has any research been conducted on the severity of autistic characteristics and distress during warmer conditions?

One final note:

At this time of year, the traditional, repetitive and comfortingly predictable school timetable gets torn up and thrown in the bin at Daniel's school, and a series of Gala swimming, performing arts programmes, award ceremonies and sports days are shoe-horned in its place.

So perhaps this regular disruption to the school routine could be, in part, to blame. In which case a lot of what I have just written could be a load of rubbish.

This just proves just HOW difficult a condition severe autism is to understand. You think you gain a glimmer of understanding and then the next minute...

A Day in the Life of Daniel...
During the School Holidays

Routine, Routine, Routine

A typical (non-school) day in the life of Daniel. We will start at midnight and Daniel is awake:

12.30 am I will periodically start to giggle, make "Aye, Aye" noises, and find suitable sound and light toy to entertain myself.

1.00 am Reach hyperactive levels and start to dismantle bed in order to climb on and off. All conducted while maintaining giggling and range of fairly audible noises.

2.30 am Start to tire of playing and become agitated and tired, get upset because bed is no longer in a position ready for sleep. Increase in agitation until Mum or Dad relent and get up to re-arrange. Get up for a nappy change and I am happy now, giggling, someone is now awake to play with. I am wet through because I wanted to move my nappy and have subsequently wet. I do this frequently and sometimes my periods of distress will accelerate quickly because I need changing. I don't like being soiled at bedtime but do not express a need to go to the toilet, nor does it bother me during the daytime.

2.40 am Back to bed and fairly happy until realisation hits that Mum or Dad are not going to stay and play. I am awake and I have run out of things to entertain me.

3.00 am Increased agitation leads to full-blown distress. Unable to get back to sleep although feeling tired and no-one present to calm. I alternate between full distress sounds and then quiet.

4.00 am Mum, Dad or both have appeared because my distress became persistent. I am very frustrated because I cannot sleep and make my feelings known by lashing out. Another nappy check, some E45 cream applied in case of itchy skin and some foot massages. Nursery rhymes and tickling games distract me and then massages help relax me.

4.30 am Left alone again, continue to make contented sounds intermingled with whines of discontent.

5.00 am Slowly noise making dies out and is replaced by sleep.

7.00 am Wake up in full-blown distress as dislike waking from a deep sleep.

7.15 am Begin to calm down again and play in bedroom.

7.30 am Time to get up, distressed again, where is my breakfast??

7.45 am Nappy changed, dressed and downstairs. Sometimes I can follow this routine quite chilled out but sometimes I can be very tearful and will head-butt. You didn't get my breakfast when I expected it, now I am having to wait for it because it wasn't on the table when I came downstairs. I will cry until my toast is ready.

7.50 am First two rounds of toast have been completed, now where is my next serving? Why was the toaster not on while I was eating? I will hand you my plate ready for some more toast. I am not happy though and my vocalisation will tell you that. My beaker is empty; you can have that too.

7.55 am Two more slices of toast demolished and another beaker of drink. Off I go to play in the living room.

8.00 am I will draw the curtains, already undrawn to let the pets out. Depending on my mood, I will either chew the curtains or go and play with the Duplo. I will sit and begin to make mirror image models. If there are any shoes lying around I may choose to play with them, particularly Velcro fastening, as they are good to chew on. If I am chewing on the curtains and my parents walk in, I will immediately run to sit down somewhere. I know that the curtains are off limits but sometimes I cannot find anything else that settles me.

8.15 am My peace has been destroyed by my two younger sisters joining me in the room. I will see if I can go out in the garden by trying the back door. The door is locked and as no-one is opening it for me, I retreat to the kitchen with some of my Lego blocks.

8.45 am I am still sitting at the table and no-one has given me anything else to eat. I have handed you my beaker and it has been refilled but I'd really like something else to eat. I will search in the cupboards myself, hmmm, mini cheddars, but oh, you have told me to go and play. Ok.

9.00 am I am back in the living room with my Lego blocks but I haven't forgotten that I want something else to eat. I am getting increasingly unsettled and would really like something to eat. I cannot go outside and the Lego is no longer entertaining me. My sisters are making a lot of noise.

9.15 am I have come back into the kitchen and given you my dinner plate. It must be approaching snack time. You have told me to go and play again, ok, but only because the back door is now open and I can go outside.

9.45 am It really must be snack time now, I am not leaving the table until you feed me and I am not happy to wait. I have got a packet of mini cheddars out of the cupboard but I need you to open them, why haven't you opened them? I wanted them open when I handed them to you and yet here we are and they are not open. Open them!

10.00 am Mini cheddars finished and refuelled for now. Off to go on the trampoline where I will spend 75% of the time chewing the net and 10% sunbathing and 15% bouncing, interspersed with spells on the slide and going in and out of the house to collect Lego and sound operated toys that I like to play with.

10.30 am Back inside for a breather and a play with the Lego or my sound toys.

11.00 am It's lunchtime, isn't it? It must be lunchtime. No??? But...

11.15 am Back in the living room with Mum or Dad and we'll have a tickling game for a few minutes and I'll let you massage my feet because I really really want my lunch and I am not happy that you haven't prepared it.

11.30 am I said I wanted my lunch. Where is it? You have only just put the oven on and I am now not going to leave the table until you serve it. I am not going to wait quietly because you didn't listen to me and now I am upset.

11.40 am Lunch is ready and I have taken a few mouthfuls of it but am now quite happy to go off and play. Lunch can wait.

11.50 am I am back to finish off my lunch having had a quick bounce on the trampoline. Then I am off to play quietly with some Lego for a few minutes.

12.00 pm My nappy needs changing but you are still eating your lunch. I will come and sit at the table because this will tell you I need my nappy changed.

12.05 pm You haven't changed my nappy and my plate is empty. I will ask for something else to eat instead. Oh you have detected that I need changing.

12.10 pm I am quite happy to have my nappy changed and feel better now, thank you. However, my plate is empty and I could eat something else so I will hover in case you have more food for me. I will hand you my plate just in case.

12.20 pm I have given up and am now quite happily playing in the garden.

3.00 pm I have been playing out in the garden and am feeling peckish. I will have a look in the cupboard again to see if I can find anything to eat. I could have some cereal and will try to get that myself. I have taken a bowl out of the cupboard and can pour the cereal myself. It is fun to put some on the table to play with too. I have noticed the chairs have not been put back correctly after lunch. I need to line the chairs up with the table.

3.30 pm Mum or Dad has taken the cereal off me and it is now approaching teatime. When I am at school, I get home around 3.30pm and expect my tea to be waiting. I am not happy because I should be eating my tea now. Mum or Dad has put the oven on and I am waiting. I don't like waiting. Where is my tea?

3.45 pm I have pizza and finish this off in a matter of minutes. I am happy to go off and play for a little while.

4.45 pm What is this? My sisters are having their tea. Where is my food? My plate is still empty? I want to sit with them and eat too. I will have some biscuits; it must be two so that I can line them up with each other.

5.00 pm I am quite happy to play now until it is time to come in which will be around 7pm. However, I have been outside a lot today and I am bored of the slide and trampoline. I will have a look in the cabin and sit on the chairs. I might sit on the grass but know Mum or Dad will move me as I have a penchant for eating mud. I will be called in for a nappy change during this play session and often will have soiled; most often I will wait until I have gone to bed though.

7.00 pm It is nearing the time I go to bed so I will come in out of the garden. No-one has taken me upstairs so I will wait at the bottom. Oh, there is the cat water bowl and it is full. I like to empty this and watch the water run on the stairs.

7.30 pm Mum or Dad is taking me up to bed. I will sit on the toilet and watch while they get my bedtime clothes ready. I have checked to make sure the bath is empty because tonight isn't bath night and sometimes baths can be very stressful for me. I am still a little anxious but I now have my nappy on so that must mean no bath tonight. I have had my face wiped and my teeth brushed. I don't like to have my face wiped or my hands washed but will tolerate this. I like the toothbrush but like to bite down on it and giggle. My pyjamas are on and it is time to go in my room. I like to have some tickle games at bedtime.

8.00 pm I am happily playing in my room but I have soiled my nappy. I won't let on just yet. My bed is on its side and my mattress is a slide. My shutters are open and I am currently upside down balanced on the window sill.

9.00 pm I am tired now. Mum or Dad has checked on me and changed my nappy. I have melatonin as I struggle to get to sleep on my own. I am quite agitated because my bed needs putting back together so I can sleep.

9.05 pm The melatonin is starting to have a result and I don't like it one bit. I get very distressed at this time of day and will cry out before going to sleep. The melatonin is natural and doesn't hurt me but I don't like the drowsy stage very much.

9.35 pm I have finally gone to sleep. Mum and Dad have checked on me again and put some E45 on my legs and I am content.

11.00 pm What was that? I heard a noise... someone on the stairs. I will make a noise so they know I am here. Mum or Dad are close by and going to bed.

12.00 pm Is it time to get up? I don't think it is but I cannot get to sleep. I have spotted a toy that looks fun to play with.

Not every night is like this but in the holidays a few things do take over for Daniel:

- Food Obsessions

- Sleep Deprivation

- Loss of Routine

We could make his bedroom completely uninteresting and take all the toys away. He is limited to only a few and those that make light or noise are for his benefit. If he becomes completely obsessed by them we do remove them temporarily, but historically, Daniel going to bed has been a place of complete terror where he was unhappy to be left alone for any length of waking time.

Daniel is currently averaging 4-6 hours of sleep per night. We are able to doze through some of his "wake" time and instinctively know when he needs us to tend to him. We don't go in for every murmur because otherwise he will expect that. Not so long ago we would be up at 2am giving him toast to try to pacify him back to sleep.

Dad and the MMR

There are advances in medicine all the time but who can say for sure what the long-term effects are? Sometimes, new and innovative doesn't make up for old and trusted.

I was put unexpectedly on the spot last week – at the surgery with youngest daughter Sophie for one of the standard childhood jabs, I think it was Tetanus, Polio and Diphtheria –when the nurse suddenly said "You realise Sophie is due her booster MMR today, don't you...?" and the little cardboard box containing said vaccine was revealed to me right there, ready and waiting to go into Sophie's arm, should I give "the nod".

By a strange coincidence the very same week, the main news on TV and in the press had been running an ongoing series of stories about a cluster of measles outbreaks occurring in Wales, blamed on the poor update of the MMR jab.

On this occasion once again, as before with my older daughter Rebecca, I couldn't bring myself to give the ok, babbling something about needing to discuss with my wife first, and trying to reassure the nurse that "we wouldn't leave Sophie unprotected". But I will admit feeling a little threatened given the recent news... and almost expected the nurse to roll her eyes and tut under her breath, thinking "here's another one of those nut-job parents who's not taking up the MMR". On this occasion I was pleasantly surprised when she didn't, instead just asking if I could let them know what we decide for their records.

But good question... why...? What on earth am I thinking refusing a vaccine for my precious daughter?

I'm far from being a medical expert, but know that the whole "MMR thing" of course, goes back to the late 1990s (1998 I think) when a Dr Wakefield (who has since been struck off and can no longer practice in the UK) published a report in a well-respected medical journal suggesting a possible link between the triple, live, measles, mumps and rubella (MMR) vaccine and the appearance of autistic symptoms in some children soon afterwards. From what I understand, he went on to suggest that the MMR vaccine should be temporarily withdrawn to allow time for further research to be conducted.

All I know above and beyond that is that Dr Wakefield's research was later "discredited" and found to be flawed (but I will openly admit to not knowing the full details of why and what the problems were), and also that "current research" does not show ANY link between the MMR vaccine and onset of autism in children.

So why not go with the flow, accept the current findings and allow Sophie the MMR booster?

The following statements are facts concerning our son Daniel...

> (i) Daniel was given the MMR jab at approximately 13 months.
>
> (ii) Daniel developed autism (later severe autism) shortly afterwards.

So, there's the proof right? No – consider the following facts about Daniel too:

> (i) Daniel ate a fish finger for the first time at 13 months.
>
> (ii) Daniel developed autism (later severe autism) shortly afterwards.

The second statement definitely proves that fish fingers cause autism... doesn't it?!

Well, of course they don't, and neither of us are naive enough to state that the MMR vaccine caused Daniel's autism either. We don't know what did. All we know was that a doctor suggested a link... and that plants a seed in your mind, a hint of uncertainty and concern. It's like an itch that won't go away. I was aware that the MMR had been given the "all clear" before Daniel had it; yet he went on to develop severe autism and learning difficulties. And as a parent who went on to have further children, you will do ANYTHING to try to prevent repeating ANY action that might have had even the remotest chance of being in some way linked to the onset of Daniel's condition. Cold hard logic doesn't always come into the equation I'm afraid. There are other factors. We started to read that some of the chemicals used in the vaccine as a preservative were under scrutiny. At one stage I believe mercury may have been used (maybe in Daniel's batch, but I'm not sure), which was later withdrawn. Both Daniel and Rebecca also had quite nasty reactions to some of their earlier vaccinations too. All of these facts play on your mind.

Despite all of this, as I said earlier we really don't know, and quite possibly never will know why Daniel developed severe autism.

One thing that's certain is that the human body and particularly the brain is IMMENSELY complex, and the world's best scientists and doctors are barely scratching at the surface where an understanding of how the human brain, the "soul" and character of each of us, our very being and self-awareness, are concerned. With the very best will in the world, "current research" is just that... "current". As time progresses, more will undoubtedly be understood and views and policies that are standard practice for the health service now will change.

For me, my belief at the moment is that autistic characteristics may be genetic in nature, i.e. you are born with them. But that some external factor possibly "triggers" the appearance of symptoms. From what I understand, the incidence of autism in boys has increased hugely in the past few decades – some of which may be attributed to the number of cases being diagnosed, but certainly not all.

So what is causing the rapid increase in cases? Scientists will continue to perform incredible work in their efforts to figure this out. But in the meantime, it seems to me that maybe bombarding a child's body with multiple live viruses and the associated chemicals and preservatives in which they are suspended just could perhaps be a trigger? For Daniel, add to the mix a long lasting round of antibiotics (taken to attempt to clear up a stubborn case of impetigo – a skin complaint beneath his hair) and perhaps some tipping point that his already genetically predisposed body could no longer cope with was passed, and it was all downhill from there.

So yes, we do continue to worry despite NHS reassurances that the MMR is perfectly safe. And we'll be booking in Sophie for her single, spaced out vaccinations, in the near future.

Change is as Good as Rest... Unless You Live in an Autism Household

Any change should be planned with the military precision of the best army, the magic potions of a wizard, and the telepathic powers of a psychic.

With three children under five and the country in the grips of recession, we made the difficult decision to move house. With the property market in the middle of a crash, the timing wasn't brilliant, but then again neither were our finances. For Daniel, this would be the fourth home in his young life. The first time he had been just five months old. It didn't really occur to me at the time but he really didn't like the sound of the packing tape being applied to the boxes. Maybe that was an early sign! The first two times had been positive moves for something bigger and better. This time was very much a case of just cheaper!

Routine is a word that comes up everywhere when managing a child with autism. Devise a routine and do not dare deviate from it or you will pay the price forevermore, or something to that effect. As things go, I would say we have been fairly lucky as although Daniel knows his routine and does have certain expectations that arise from it, he CAN (I say, hesitantly) be quite accepting if things don't always go to plan. That said, along with routine comes the word 'change'. This can be much more problematic and especially so when the change is permanent. Change is a difficult concept for someone on the autistic spectrum and something that we have to find a way to explain to Daniel. There have been numerous occasions where we have temporarily rearranged furniture for family visits or birthday gatherings, only to find Daniel in the midst of rearranging it back to how it was before.

We had initially had the discussion about moving house shortly after I went on maternity leave with Sophie, going as far as having the house valued and preliminary photos taken. However, at the time, we were so torn between our beautiful house and the reality that faced us. At this point we were not sure whether I would be able to go back to work full-time. Mike had just started to return to site work, which meant overseas travel for weeks on end. With three children with very different needs and no sleep at night, one of us needed to be at home. Indeed, we made the very difficult decision to let our nanny go and instead employed someone on a part-time basis.

This worked to start with but life was certainly challenging and finances were still incredibly tough. Our home, initially chosen because of its rural location, began to show how isolating it was and we desperately needed to be closer to support services and most importantly work. The time to commute became wearing. Part-time work just wasn't paying the bills either and by the end of the year, two things had to change: I had to go back to work full-time and we needed to downsize our home. At this point, our old nanny came back to join us and we set about finding somewhere for us all to live that factored in the multitude of needs.

In May of the following year, we finally completed the house sale. The sale had not gone smoothly and the relief that it was finally happening was immense. That said, we were incredibly nervous as to how Daniel would take to it. This time we were not just rearranging the furniture; we were rearranging it and setting it back down in completing new surroundings. Daniel had continued to be up and down but ultimately not to the same degree as the previous summer. Daniel surpassed all our expectations and coped incredibly well with the move, actually sleeping well and being quite happy and sociable in the new house. That is until about three weeks after the move.

Those next three weeks that followed were the worst we have experienced (to date) with Daniel and on this occasion medication did see us turn a corner. This involved two trips to A&E to rule out pain because Daniel didn't stop crying for days and weeks, wouldn't eat, and just became a shadow of his former self. However, this wasn't without some absolutely dreadful experiences. We were prescribed a series of medications such as Piriton to help get Daniel to sleep and codeine to rule out pain. Daniel at this point was suspected to have toothache. A routine dentist appointment had discovered some problems with decay caused by overcrowding but because of his diagnosis, he would need a general anaesthetic to remove some milk teeth. Of course this doesn't happen overnight but we were told it would be at least six months. Six months with toothache just isn't on so we did everything we could to try to get this brought forward.

Traditional painkillers were not touching whatever it was. If anything Daniel already had an issue with paracetamol suspension because it made him incredibly hyperactive. In the end codeine was prescribed, but let's just say that unless it is a life or death matter, I will NOT be allowing him to have codeine again. The aggression and turmoil was unbearable.

Finally, we managed to get an emergency call to a paediatrician who suspected that this was not in fact in pain related – well, not pain of a physical nature. To get to this conclusion, she asked a lot of questions about the time leading up to the downturn and what we usually did to manage Daniel when he was upset, and suggested other techniques to calm him. She felt that Daniel was suffering a delayed reaction to the house move. Indeed, he spent a lot of his waking time trying to get out of the house, something he had never really tried before! He refused to go in the back garden, having happily bounced on his relocated trampoline days before. The behaviours Daniel was presenting were a sign of mental anguish and his system had gone into overload.

To explain, Daniel had been more than happy to investigate his new surroundings and sleep in his new bedroom, almost too happy, but in his mind this was not a permanent arrangement. Once it became apparent that we were going to be staying in this new dwelling, the anxiety set in and with it came the mother of all meltdowns. Once again we found ourselves in a position where the only solution seemed to be to medicate and things were getting desperate. Daniel was prescribed risperidone.

Risperidone is an anti-psychotic drug used for the treatment of schizophrenia and bipolar disorder. The side effects were plentiful and we witnessed them in all their glory. Daniel developed a penchant for swinging his arms constantly, unable to control himself. He went off into his own little world, completely impenetrable, focussed only on biting the inside of his mouth and his bedding was covered in blood and this was the side effect. When he finally went to sleep that night we vowed that he wasn't to take another dose BUT then he did something he hadn't done for weeks... SLEPT and when he woke up in the morning he was calm and he ate.

With further discussion with the paediatrician we were able to lower the dose and with the help of daily ibuprofen (to rule out tooth pain) things started to get back on track. Daniel was much calmer but the side effects we had to witness him experience were heart-breaking and eventually we decided to wean him off it some six weeks later. I think it was almost certainly a delayed reaction to the house move and ultimately the risperidone broke the cycle. However, without doubt I think that paediatrician who took the time to listen, monitored Daniel's progress on medication and suggested other things to try, made us aware that we were not alone, and gave us offers of help (we accepted them) played a vital role because once we started to calm down, so did Daniel.

They say that with all these drugs you will see a miraculous change (over time) or no change at all. If Daniel's anguish increased to a level where he was a danger to himself or others, then we would be foolish not to seek advice, but rather than see medication as the absolute answer, I'd be looking more at what is the question, and can this be answered another way? As a parent, I have been too quick to jump on an opportunity to solve a problem without necessarily considering all the options. If you are witnessing your child in distress, ANYTHING is better than nothing, at least at the time. These drugs can and do change lives for some individuals and for this, we have to give credit where it is due.

We have got to the point where we can be very nervous when Daniel is put on medication because we just don't know how it is going to go with him. Once upon a time we'd have blind faith that a prescription was the answer, and get very downhearted when it didn't work or made things worse. These days, I think it is okay to be cautious and voice our concerns. We are not all built the same. There is just so much we still have to learn about our child and we have to accept that there isn't going to be a miracle cure.

So yes, we are a little apprehensive to change but sometimes it is unavoidable. Ultimately experience has taught us that these storms do pass but you can't help but feel a little older and silver-haired as result.

Is it Me?

Was it something I did... or didn't do?

Is it me? This is a question that I can almost certainly guarantee will have entered into the mind of every parent faced with his or her child's diagnosis of autism. Is it me? Was it something I did? Am I on the spectrum?

Well everyone is on the spectrum somewhere and as you learn to live with a child's diagnosis of autism, you will find there is no such thing as typical. In your neuro-typical (NT) child you will see "autistic" behaviours. In the person walking down the street you will see mannerisms that make you think twice.

When Daniel was first diagnosed, we researched and read everything. Using the internet as our main resource led to a whole host of differing emotions: alarm, fear, heartbreak, motivation, reassurance and guilt.

Guilt leads us back to "Is it me?" The list of supposed links to autism is endless and as a parent you cannot help but feel responsible.

Then there is grief! You start to read up on statistics such as 'over 50% of those diagnosed with autism require specialist life-long support and a further 30% require support of some kind to live independently'. No one can say at the time of diagnosis whether your child will be one of the 20% and even if they were, whether quality of life would be affected by the increased risk of bullying, from vulnerability or aggressive behaviours. So at some point, it is likely that some sort of grieving will take place, for all the hopes and ambitions you held for your child. Please rest assured that by admitting this, it doesn't mean we have given up on our son, but our hopes and aspirations for him have changed.

Ok, so back to "Is it me?" Almost everything all research will mention is that there is a genetic link and that a history of autism in the family will increase the chances of further offspring being on the spectrum. Well, for us, there is no history of autism diagnosis noted on either side BUT higher functioning autism often goes undiagnosed. So although Daniel's lower functioning autism is evident and marked by learning disability, for those who are higher functioning, it may not have been recognised as such. We have a history of autoimmune conditions on both sides and current studies are investigating whether autism can be linked to autoimmune conditions or even classed as one itself. It is relevant to say that it is not yet fully understood what leads to the onset of autoimmune conditions either (diabetes type 1, multiple sclerosis).

Aside from genetic factors, you also find out there are environmental factors that are linked to autism. These include overload of metals in drinking water, use of wireless technology, and exposure to chemicals. With Daniel being our firstborn, I followed religiously every piece of advice given to an expectant mum. I sacrificed my peanut butter, I didn't drink diet drinks, and I restricted my intake of tuna. I can't rule out environmental factors but I did my best.

Then there is the research stating that breastfeeding reduces the incidence of autism diagnosis and refrigerator mums have been linked to autistic behaviours. The implication is that parenting which does not include showering your child with love and affection increases the incidence of autism. Of course, I recognise why a starvation of love may lead to a distant and disconnected child, but our little boy spent the first eight months of life physically attached to me or being held by another member of the family for much of the time. When he wasn't being breastfed, he was enjoying a cuddle with Mum, being bounced and burped by Dad, and generally receiving a whole load of loving from family.

This leads back to "Is it me?" After you have considered all options, you tend to start looking at yourself and yes, I have wondered, since Daniel's diagnosis, if I too am on the spectrum.

There has always been this feeling that I do not fit in, a social awkwardness that has been with me since childhood. On the face of it, it is shyness and there are still instances now when I have been reprimanded for being too quiet. There are others I am sure who would also like me to shut up!

As I have gotten older, I have become more confident in initiating a conversation or making contact but still struggle with knowing when it is my turn to speak. This can be particularly problematic in larger groups and I can feel myself withdraw. I am wary of appearing self-absorbed because I struggle to open a conversation but will respond if asked about myself.

Then you look again and realise we all have our strengths and weaknesses and our son, yes he has an autism diagnosis, but he is still a little boy and it is just one facet of his being, like his brown eyes, the knowing look when he is about to do something he shouldn't, and his infectious giggle. I can't honestly say the "Is it me?" days will ever completely leave us behind. There will be research, I'm sure, that will make us question past actions. However, it doesn't stop us from making the most of life as it is.

Funny, You're the Broken One, but I'm the Only One Who Needed Saving

For some, awareness of their disability is negligible. However, for those around them it is painfully obvious.

Given the worryingly high proportions of children affected by autism spectrum disorders in recent years, there are, as you might expect, a multitude of support groups for affected families – both online, in terms of websites and Facebook pages/groups, and similar, various levels of groups that meet up, both at a regional and neighbourhood/local level, and charities such as the National Autistic Society in the UK. These groups provide a crucial lifeline to struggling families – both in terms of help – practical suggestions, contact details where support can be provided, helpline phone numbers and email addresses – but perhaps most importantly of all, a place where parents can get to meet others who *truly* understand how difficult it can be looking after and guiding an autistic child through life's journey.

For me, personally – I'm going to own up now, and say that I have tended to only rarely attend the regular support group meetings covering the area where we live. And why is that? Well, first things first – I am not in any way shape or form going to criticise these support groups, which are so important for many people. Far from it, for many I know these are a lifeline! My view, though – if you're going to spend a sizeable chunk of your time, day after day, month after month, toiling hard to raise a child with a significant disability, do you necessarily want to spend some precious time *away* from all of that talking about the very same thing?! Respite is possibly one of the most important things that has allowed us to survive and maintain something approaching sanity over the years – so an evening off? We're more likely head out for a Chinese buffet or carvery and a relaxing drink, and very nice too... but that's just us. Perhaps we always were socially awkward in that way... Perhaps if respite breaks were thrown our way on a frequent basis – then I suspect we would more likely try to attend.

That said, we most certainly do maintain a close eye on support groups via social networking such as Facebook.

Social networking sites in recent times have themselves come under a lot of criticism. In recent days there has been a huge wave of quite understandable negative publicity concerning the social network site "ask.fm", whereby a lot of highly unpleasant and unsavoury comments have been targeted at younger members, in a few cases even leading to the desperately sad situation where suicides have occurred.

I have also noticed a trend whereby any online news articles concerning Facebook or similar social networks appear to immediately encourage a wave of hostile comments from readers, stating not only that they will *never* subscribe to such a service but that those who do are complete sad losers with no life and no friends in the "real world".

Why on earth such people cannot be satisfied with saying that it's "not for them" and leave it at that is beyond me. I wonder – I suspect most people who come out with these comments have friends, relations, nieces, nephews and other contacts that do regularly tweet or post online – are they saying they are sad losers too?

In the world of the autism support group, what I see very frequently is the exact opposite of what has been described. To me these pages are a marvel – to think that there is somewhere you can raise a concern, or say that you are struggling, or you are alone, that you can't cope – and have someone who not only understands precisely where you are coming from, who is quite possibly in the same boat as you BUT could be almost anywhere in the world, respond with genuine words of support and kindness and understanding, that is an amazing thing. And in the world of Facebook, when someone posts, you genuinely may not have any idea of their background, age, colour, whether they are wealthy or poor... only that they have taken the time to be supportive and understanding during your time of need. Surely that's not a bad thing?

People who look after children with autism simply may not have the respite available to them, may very well not have the money, and almost certainly will not always have the energy to go out to pubs, parties, dinners, weddings and other social events. Sadly we have run into the situation ourselves where we have politely turned down wedding invitations or other social events. This very weekend coming up, we have been invited to a christening some three or four hours' drive from here. Alas, with no respite available over the holiday weekend, it's looking like I will attend with my daughter, leaving my wife at home to care for Daniel. One thing I guarantee we can do each and every day, however, is enjoy the contact and shared thoughts, jokes and messages with others in the online community.

I like to think that, for every unkind or hurtful message posted to individuals via social networking – and let's hope this kind of behaviour can be curbed – there are thousands more messages sent of support, concern, advice and understanding via these sites, and maybe someone who felt a bit low, tired or very alone in the world logs off feeling happier, understood and no longer alone.

And with that closing thought, once I've finished composing these thoughts, I will log on and see what else is happening in Facebook this evening. After all, the kids are in bed so we're not going out just now...

Autism and the Seven Dwarfs

Grumpy visits more than we would like

A little fairy story except this does not liken to a Disney cinematic feature, but is instead closer to Columbia Pictures' 1993 film 'Groundhog Day'.

Based loosely around 'Snow White and the Seven Dwarfs', I present to you 'Autism and the Seven Dwarfs'. Sadly there is no Snow White although some would say that a wicked witch appears frequently...

Indeed, there are not seven dwarfs either but rather one miniature man taking lead role. In conversation earlier this week, it occurred to me that Daniel often adopts the persona of each of the seven dwarfs and can interchange between all within a blink of an eye.

So introducing the cast:

Sneezy – Sneezy was one of the first dwarfs introduced to us when, as a fairly young baby, it became apparent that Daniel suffered from allergies. Tummy upsets, cramps and eczema dominated a long time before autism took over.

Happy – Daniel was a happy baby for the most part as long as his tummy was full and his bottom dry. I recall trips around supermarkets with him in full smiley beam as a chunky toddler. These days supermarkets are overwhelming and somewhat frightening for Daniel as the comfort of sitting securely in the trolley has long passed. However, back then and even now, he still has the most wonderful smile. When Daniel is happy, it is like a huge cloud lifts and you cannot help but smile when he giggles.

Sleepy – Well, sleepy is something Daniel often isn't. He suffers with major sleep issues and we are all often sleep deprived. That said, when he IS asleep and you need to wake him, usually a school day, oh boy do you have a fight on your hands. He will bury himself in his duvet and steadfastly refuse to move. Once you have woken him from his slumber, expect to meet another dwarf or two... Dopey and Grumpy!!

Dopey – Dopey visits on those mornings when Daniel just doesn't want to get up. He will sit at the breakfast table, surrounded by his requisite toast and rice milk, with a completely vacant expression. He will seem oblivious to his surroundings. This isn't the only time when Dopey visits. Occasionally Daniel will have absent episodes, quite common in the autism world where he zones out and becomes unaware of anyone else. These have lessened as he has grown but in 'down' periods can be the precursor for Daniel when he is anxious or about to become distressed.

Grumpy – Grumpy visits more than we would like. With the uncertainty of the day, Grumpy includes spells of crying and self-harming. It is extremely rare for Daniel to go a whole day without Grumpy appearing. As I write, Grumpy has made an appearance. Lots of tears and all the nursery rhymes, pressure squashes and massages are greeted with attempted head-butts. You can end up feeling as though you have been through a round in a boxing ring. All will go quiet and then five minutes later it all starts again.

Bashful – The wiki encyclopaedia describes Bashful dwarf as shy, sweet, nervous, irrepressible, funny, cute, gentle and easily flustered. Daniel holds all of these qualities in varying doses but it is fair to say you have to understand him before you can fully appreciate how they feature.

Doc – Doc is described as the leader of the dwarfs and in our household this is certainly true of Daniel. Although we try to ensure the needs of the whole family are met, we cannot do this without first ensuring Daniel is content and happy. The name 'Doc' could also translate to all things medical. Daniel has certainly seen his fair share of doctors over the years in the form of GPs, paediatricians, audiologists for hearing, orthoptists for sight, ophthalmologists for sight, a cardiologist for suspected heart murmur (none found), pathology for various genetic and routine testing, urology and incontinence teams, hospital dentistry, occupational therapy, speech and language therapy, education psychologists, clinical psychologists, Casualty for trying to eat a toilet block and further distress episodes. Oh, and dieticians and DAN (defeat autism now) doctors.

Daniel has had tests or treatment at numerous hospitals, at least five different ones in the southeast of England. If nothing else, Mummy and Daddy have increased knowledge of the local hospital infrastructure.

And so with introducing the leading cast, there is no time for the actual fairy tale. However, we see all these dwarfs daily, sometimes hourly or all at the same time. We strive for a happy ending!

To Have a Clone or Eyes in the Back of One's Head

By now, I am thinking it really must be a full moon or something.

So as a working mummy, I have just returned for the last hour before the piglets' bedtime to spend some time with the little darlings (cue nervous laugh).

The phone rings and I have to take the call. In the space of five minutes Daniel has helped himself to a box of cocoa pops and is halfway through tipping them out onto the dining room table. He has emptied the cat water bowl all over the carpeted stairs and is happily munching on the cocoa pops and simultaneously tipping out his Ribena juice on the table and kitchen floor.

As Daniel has managed to open the cupboard, one of his smaller partners in crime has helped themselves to the remaining Jaffa Cakes. After I clear up said mess, the phone rings again and I answer. This time I have two girls climbing over me (Rebecca and Sophie) as I try to listen and also explain that I need to supervise the cocoa pop monster.

So, finally free of the phone and said monkey pigs, I venture back into the kitchen to find Daniel has turned on the taps and is flicking water across the kitchen... cue bedtime.

Daniel, still full of mischief, decides to play around instead of getting ready for bed, more tap turning on and off, when suddenly he decides to put his hand down the toilet!!!

I breathe a sigh of relief when Daniel is safely concealed in his room. I glance in as I make my way for the stairs. Daniel is currently hanging upside down with his bed base on its side with the mattress precariously balanced as a makeshift slide.

If you ever phone us and we do not answer, please do not take it personally. We may be fighting floodwaters or wading through sticky rivers and cocoa pop mountains.

"This"

There are countless ways in which one can make a sound, or make noise. You can sing, chant, whistle or warble. Alternatively, you could wail, whine, chirrup or hum. Or how about good old screaming, shrieking, yelling or growling? A good old laugh and giggle are probably a nicer way of producing sound. Yes, there are myriad ways to disrupt the peace.

Or... you could talk.

Daniel has become an expert at fourteen of the fifteen methods described above. I'd say that is a pretty impressive record... isn't it? Daniel's two sisters have so far failed to come anywhere near close to equalling his mastery of the whistled tune or warble. And when upset, Daniel has correctly identified the precise combination of frequencies that sound the most wretched and miserable to the human ear – and successfully creates all of them simultaneously. It's no mean feat.

The trouble is, the only one he cannot (or is that won't?) get to grips with is talking. Which, let's face it, can pose a little bit of a problem – since talking represents the primary method of successful face-to-face communication between people. So how *do* we communicate with Daniel? How have we managed to function throughout his life so far, without the use of any two-way exchanges by use of speech? It's a sad fact that, like so many others who develop autism as a young child, Daniel was *oh so close* to developing speech, but lost everything during his regression around the age of two. We tantalisingly heard babbling that approximated 'Dadda' and 'Doggy' and a handful of other simple words. There were even perfectly recognisable attempts at kids' TV themes, such as 'Balamory'. How cruel to hear these – we even have some short video snippets for evidence – then realise that all were gradually lost. They have never returned.

As parents I can only say that when it happened, we knew something was up. We knew he was regressing, in the way that only a child's mum and dad can. It wasn't just the speech; it was the disassociation with his environment, his surroundings and his close family. The blank stares into space, the non-existent need to eagerly point out anything to us, like a bird on a wall, a bus driving along the street, an exciting toy. We listened as friends and family assured us that all would be well – how a little boy that so-and-so knows didn't talk until they were three and numerous similar tales. We maintained our hopes outwardly, but inside were coming to terms with a potential life without speech.

What this doesn't mean is that we stop talking to Daniel ourselves – and it has been constantly recommended throughout his life that we continue to address him, albeit via very short sentences. Daniel understands a wide number of phrases. How about this for a VERY clearly understood one – and something he shares with most other little boys.

"Daniel... DINNERTIME..." Food is always a good motivator.

Many others are fully understood, typically preceded by his name. 'Shoes on' or 'bedtime', for instance.

These, however, are just simple statements. Anything more complex or requiring a response are a different matter. We constantly find ourselves asking questions of him that he cannot answer by use of speech. "What is it, why are you upset, Daniel?" "If you don't want toast, what *would* you like to eat?" "What do you want me to get for you – is it something from the kitchen cupboard?"

The good news is that speech represents only one of a multitude of communication methods, so we have other options up our sleeve as we try to understand our son, regardless of how tough they often prove to be! At the simplest level, this is achieved by sound. (The wretched growling sounds mentioned previously, in all likelihood, mean Daniel is not happy with something.) Gestures are also vitally important. If Daniel waves his drinks beaker in your face accompanied with disgruntled noises, there is a good chance he wants his drink topped up. If he's expected to go somewhere, yet drops to the floor crying, one could probably make the assumption that he doesn't want to go! So, we are able to stumble and stagger our way through life listening to sounds, *tones* and gestures, the best we can.

What we can't do is figure out the subtler, precise answers to questions. If Daniel has a toothache, or a sore throat, there really is no precise way of knowing.

There are, however, real and proven techniques used for communication with non-verbal children. The two main ones we have encountered so far are PECS ('Picture Exchange Communication System') and Makaton (Signing). Alas, so far our efforts to implement either system have met with severely limited success with Daniel. PECS was introduced to us as a concept when Daniel was still at pre-school age – the aim being for the child to exchange a picture of a simple image, be it an item of food, drinks beaker or whatever, with an adult. The adult then provides the item requested. If the child 'gets it', the complexity and number of images can be increased, effectively increasing the vocabulary for the child and providing an increasingly effective means of communicating their needs. So far, despite persistence over several years, Daniel is still at the most basic stage with PECS – barely understanding the idea that a picture can be exchanged for something, and not really able to discriminate when the images depict more than one item.

Makaton's big advantage is that no 'items' are required to sign, no pictures, no Velcro-covered boards to carry around. Many of us lucky enough to watch children's TV channel 'CBeebies' in the UK will be aware of Mr. Tumble communicating throughout his TV shows, by talking and continually gesticulating and waving his arms and hands around... this is actually Makaton, and every word uttered by Mr. Tumble has an equivalent hand signal or gesture associated with it. Daniel has what one might call an extremely limited vocabulary in Makaton – well, if one gesture can be called a vocabulary, that is. (Hey, it's almost as much as my knowledge of German, and I've spent some twenty weeks or so in the Frankfurt area during my adult life – so who am I to criticise?) It's an important one though – and means 'please' or 'thank you'. We do like our children to be well mannered after all...

So, with Daniel's communication limitations so painstakingly evident during his early years, we watched and we watched when Rebecca was a little baby girl... would she be able to talk? Would she be able to communicate and interact with us? Would she be aware of her surroundings, and revel in an ability to point out everyday things that she found interesting or exciting?

Thus came the delightful moment for us – the relief, and the title of this chapter – when Rebecca would, in one fell swoop, demonstrate no less than THREE actions of communication that have deserted our little boy all this time.

She sees an exciting object...
Points at it (1)...
Looks right at one of us (2)...
Utters the word "THIS!!" (3).

These simple actions, in our world, were never taken for granted – and should never BE taken for granted.

Sibling Superheroes

Daniel's condition will always make him, and by association his siblings, a target.

Daniel is big brother to two little sisters. We have brown-eyed, strawberry blond Rebecca who is eighteen months younger, and blue-eyed, blond Sophie, five years younger.

You hear these wonderful stories of siblings who love their brother/sister with autism unconditionally and accept them as they are. I would have said until quite recently that we had some way to go with this. However, I think the feelings expressed at that stage will lead to a comprehensive understanding and both girls are already an invaluable support.

Rebecca, fully aware that her brother has autism, often takes the full brunt of his frustration. Being of similar size and most likely to react, Daniel is known to give his sister a smack or two when in a temper. You will see Rebecca get up and move her breakfast (a volatile time for Daniel) resigned to the fact that if she doesn't she is in his path. Daniel also used to push his toddling sister over, cause and effect, one push and over she toppled, but I suspect this has little to do with his diagnosis...

Anyone who knows Rebecca will get that she likes to take charge so if we ask her to check on Daniel, she will happily report if he is up to something he shouldn't be: raiding the cupboard or fridge, chewing pens. Although this may seem trivial, this extra set of eyes and ears can be invaluable when we have to step out of the room. Daniel ideally needs constant supervision and is known to take such opportunities to indulge in behaviours that we would not be allowing if we were present.

Rebecca used to struggle with the fact that Daniel didn't have to tidy up, is helped to get his clothes on, gets away with not eating his dinner, stops her from being able to go out, or gets upset when we all go out together. As she has matured she is much more tolerant, yet trying to teach her one set of ideals while her sibling followed another was a challenge. Sometimes Daniel gets away with something "naughty" because a stern voice or removing a toy will simply escalate into a situation with distress that is far more challenging than the initial crime. Then there is the explaining that what is deemed as "naughty" isn't actually being "naughty" when you have no concept of the word. So yes, contempt has been there for good reason BUT, just sometimes, you'll see them play together either on the trampoline or in the house, laughing and giggling.

Sophie is much more indifferent to her brother's diagnosis. She is too young to understand autism in its entirety but follows her big sister's lead. "Mummy, Daniel is chewing the curtains", "Mummy, Daniel has done a poo" (any opportunity for talking poop), "Mummy, Daniel is being naughty".

Daniel has always been tolerant of his youngest sister, only having a few minor incidents, particularly in the early months (Daniel did NOT take kindly to the baby cry or this thing that was permanently with Mummy and Daddy), but now the two live quite happily along-side each other.

I would say that the children have a fairly typical sibling relation-ship. A lot of disagreements are nothing out of the ordinary and it is really a case of picking themselves up and moving on. There are challenges though that other children may not face and this can make it difficult for them to discuss with peers. Daniel is still in nappies. Right there you have an example of something that other children would find odd. Another example: going to the local park, we generally have to hold Daniel's hand and he will carry a chewy toy. This is something that he chews on and helps distract him when in a new or busy environment. As Daniel's age approaches double figures, the hand holding and unusual gait tend to make him stand out in a crowd. During his time at the park he is prone to upset as, although he loves the park, the unpredictability of others can make it overwhelming.

The park is one of the few places that Daniel will tolerate, so aside from it being difficult, the places where we can go out as a family are incredibly limited. As a rule we don't! These days Daniel has activities of his own and this gives us respite and the opportunity to do something that the girls want to do. However, there were a number of years where we didn't leave the house at weekends or, if we did, it would involve one of us staying behind with Daniel.

We have always tried to openly talk about Daniel and his struggles. As Rebecca gets older she is more accustomed to doing this but there is always the fear that disclosure will lead to bullying. The sad fact of the world is that this is a risk. Ignorance, fear, boredom, and spite are all potential sources of animosity.

To ensure that Rebecca doesn't bottle things up, she attends a sibling support group where she can go for a few hours and have fun, and talk about some of the struggles at home with other siblings who get it. Sophie isn't at an age yet where she can attend but should she want to go, we will encourage it.

I guess we never expected to be asking our seven-year-old daughter to go fetch a nappy (diaper) for her nine-year-old brother. Finding the humour in the situation, on one occasion she did so in giggles, not because of Daniel's need for one but because they were pink. With the teenage years not too far ahead in the future, we can only hope that amusement doesn't turn into embarrassment, but when the girls become more self-aware, it is an issue I am sure we will have to face.

As a mummy of two little girls, it is fairly commonplace to overhear bickering about who is to blame and for what. It is usually Sophie to blame and Rebecca the one blaming. Just now Daniel was getting quite upset waiting for his tea and the girls are arguing out in the other room which of them is to blame for his upset. On this occasion it is neither and I am not sure whether to be pleased that they recognise they do things that upset Daniel or sad that they need to be thinking about things that typically another child wouldn't be bothered by.

Autism diagnosis is becoming more and more common. As the next generation grows, I hope that ignorance lessens, but sadly there will always be some prejudice. Our girls have experienced challenging times in their developing years. It is our responsibility to turn that into a positive, an education that life is not always easy or straightforward, that we are not all the same but at some point we all need support.

There's a Monster in My Wardrobe

His monsters are with him all the time.

The world of the typical almost four-year-old is a whirlwind of emotion and chaos. The development of the creative mind begins to take great strides both physically and mentally. Of our three children, Sophie is the most 'inventive', equipped with an imagination far exceeding her years and acting skills RADA members would be envious of. This skill presents itself mainly in the form of 'fibs' or 'half-truths' that she can tell while looking you straight in the eye. Daniel does not possess the ability to lie and Rebecca has 'I am hiding something' written all over her face before her guilt gets to be too much and she comes clean.

Yesterday, having spent a short while attempting to tidy Sophie's room, or more fitting, attempting to find the floor amongst the chaos, I was somewhat put out to find that in no time at all, it had been trashed again. Sophie had been out at playgroup for most of the day but still had managed to undo my work in about 30 minutes of arriving home. When I questioned her, she told me quite matter-of-factly that it was not her who had messed her room, but the monster hiding behind the wardrobe. Taken aback by how easily she had told this tale, I promptly told her to tidy up. Of course it is often quite amusing, and attempting to keep a straight face I explained that she must not tell fibs or one day she will be telling the truth and no-one will believe her.

This, of course, went in one ear and came out the other. Not long after, the discovery that both her beloved piglets had drawn-on whiskers came to light. Knowing that Sophie was the only one possibly responsible, I decided to ask both Sophie and Rebecca. Rebecca indignantly stated, "Well, it wasn't me." Sophie said, "Well, it wasn't me either". Hmmm...

I made a mental note that we need to instil into Sophie that lying is no-no, and the afternoon progressed. As Daniel was out with his PA, the girls were playing 'cafe' in the living room. As time went on, I advised them that they needed to clear up as Daniel was due home and some of the toys needed to go back in their bedrooms. With this, Sophie started to cry. It transpires that Sophie was actually convinced that there was a monster in her wardrobe. I overheard Sophie explain to Rebecca that she had a dream the previous night and the monster had come out of her dreams and was now sleeping in the wardrobe. Now, Sophie isn't keen on clear up time, but the conviction in her voice and tears indicated a genuine fear.

Later on, the situation escalated with Sophie in floods of tears, reluctant to go to sleep because the 'monster's shadow was moving behind the wardrobe'. No reassurances from Mummy, Daddy or Rebecca would convince her otherwise and we had to wait for her to literally drop from tiredness. I am probably more sympathetic to her plight in this scenario. As a young child, my dad would also have to go through the nightly routine of sitting on the floor until I dropped off to sleep. I can still recall the terror I felt regarding one picture that hung in my room and even now, my vivid imagination can still leave me easily spooked at night.

It makes me wonder where imagination stops and reality starts in the eyes of a four-year-old, or does this loveable bundle of mischief just have her parents wrapped around her little finger? Daniel has suffered with sleep issues from a young age. At one point we think that he too might suffer from night terrors. He would wake up in the middle of the night with unexplained distress that left us puzzled. He has always suffered with mysterious tummy aches but this was something else.

Can you imagine waking up in fear and not being able to explain to anyone what it is that frightened you? Well, Daniel isn't any different in that he will still experience dream sleep that he will find disturbing. The only difference is that he cannot tell us what it is. But Daniel's occurrences of fear and anxiety in his waking hours are far greater than at night so these monsters lurk all the time, making reality a much scarier place for him. We can only second guess in hope that we can make it better.

1 in 5 kids with an autistic sibling show subtle symptoms too. Sibling support is as necessary as them for the directly affected.

Great Expectations
(or why expectations aren't so great!)

On a bad day, you wouldn't
wish this on your worst enemy.

So, as a rule, I believe most if not all who enter into a marriage believe it is going to be forever. Indeed, the traditional vows say 'til death do us part'. However, I wonder how many people have really thought through the consequences of 'for richer, for poorer, in sickness and in health' or how this union will work under the premise that you have 'accepted children lovingly from God' as is sometimes included in the Catholic recitation. Now promises differ from marriage to marriage but the common factor is that promises are made and they're to be kept.

So, we have been married just over ten years. I would say we are happily married. That said, we have had to face some pretty hairy times and we have experienced a number of negative life-changing events. Through that time, our marriage has stayed strong and the only thing that really has had repercussions is insecurity. If I am honest, predominantly mine.

Living with a child with autism can lead to the depths of despair and beyond, particularly when you are sleep deprived. Every day can seem eerily the same and you lose sight of your former self. This is on a bad day; NOT every day is like this but these days do and can occur. The divorce statistics for parents are high. Add autistic children and they are incredibly high. The number of single parents facing this situation alone is shocking, and for them I have the upmost admiration.

Mums and dads do walk away from their families because of a diagnosis of autism, fact!

The other thing to fall by the wayside is friends. You certainly find out who your real friends are. Your ability to be a friend diminishes because sometimes you have to cancel meet-ups because you are needed at home, or you avoid going for a night out because the need to sleep is greater. People stop asking and slowly you find it is just your family unit that you can rely on.

A typical day will see you turning into a detective with a new daily agenda as you try to fathom what triggered the latest meltdown or what has caused your son to refuse to eat, where a new behaviour has originated from and if it's a learnt behaviour, a copied behaviour or a general result of frustration. Therefore, where you might have once gone about your day-to-day business everything becomes questionable and this includes the actions and behaviours of those around you, even when there is nothing to question. Over the years, concerns have been raised about both of Daniel's siblings because we struggle to distinguish between a typical behaviour and one that needs further investigation.

On a bad day, you wonder whether you are being punished for some previous ill. The feeling that you are trapped can be all-consuming and you can literally feel like life has been snatched from you. Indeed, there have been days we have not been able to eat, sleep or leave the house, and you wonder whether conditions in jail may be more favourable. I would be lying if I said that there hasn't been a time where one or both of us have indicated, 'I can't do this anymore, I can't cope' or 'I want out', although the feeling the diminishes as quickly as it materialises. Ironically, you gain strength from those moments of despair, and by admitting to them, even more so. Even superheroes have sidekicks to help them. We both love our son without question but you simply cannot sugar-coat how living with the effects of autism can sometimes make you feel.

This is where you need respite, to turn to someone outside the unit, not already caught up in the drama that is going on at home, inside your head or wherever. The thing I have been guilty of is being involved in a situation that is intolerable and automatically assuming that Mike must be looking for a way out. Seriously, why would you want to put up with this? Insecurity comes from an irrational expectation and is the worst of all feelings. You see, talking to someone outside the situation is an escape, a respite. The grass *can* look greener when you are not faced with the groundhog experience that autism brings but ultimately only if your existing life has nothing else to offer you.

The flip side of isolation is the feeling of exposure. Sometimes it can feel like we are on stage and our performance is up there for criticism. From the number of agencies to the number of opinions you encounter, all significant when you are dealing with someone with a lifelong disability. Although a lot want to help, they ultimately have an expectation of you as well. Life can be one long appointment with tasks and deadlines to meet. How we live seems to be an open topic for conversation, often under scrutiny and it feels like we are not free to make decisions on own accord for fear it will have repercussions elsewhere. Sometimes, it would just be nice to hear that we are doing okay, a pat on the back. We have had to change our expectations of our life together and we can only hope others follow suit.

I think it is a mistake that lots of couples make when they have children. You become parents first and a couple second. Family matters dominate. You lose sight of what brought you together in the first place. Yes, for many marriage is pre-cursor to starting or confirming a family unit, but it is equally spending life experiences together. Life experiences do not consist entirely of earning the bread, housekeeping and child rearing. Time has to be made to laugh, have fun, affection, and intimacy. It isn't a luxury or being selfish. It's more like finding a balance. BUT, it is a necessity. When you add autism into the mix, it is a lifeline!

This is where I feel we lack. As a couple, we rarely get any time off with just the two of us. If we do, it is usually attending an appointment or dealing with whatever the current crisis is. Ok, with three children, we kind of abandoned any option of the free-spirited lifestyle. That was our choice and not one we regret, not at all. Watching your own family grow is an adventure in itself. However, the two individuals who made that happen still exist. That relationship still matters. We are still young and still relatively early on in our life journey. We need this space to grow, to discover for ourselves, find our own path and learn from our own mistakes. Those outsides forces I mentioned earlier with the unrealistic expectations, well, they can be the tipping point from just about managing. There are times where we have to be able to say 'NO!' and just have time to concentrate on each other and our little family... we do not exist just for the sake of others.

The upshot is that when things are bad, we do need others around us to keep us grounded, to soothe our wounds and offer support. Equally, we need the time and space to nurture our family unit, to help each other to get through. I have wasted far too much of my life worrying about what might happen, what people think and trying to find a problem where one might not exist. Our destination is unknown. The path is not one we expected to travel but expectation doesn't always bear fruit so here's to embracing our journey, wherever it may lead. The only thing good about expectations is to expect the unexpected...

Why Do We Insist on Living Here?

It certainly isn't for the weather.

All right, there's no point trying to dress this up, or skirt around the topic, so I will get straight to the point; this is going to be a rant about the weather in Britain. It shouldn't be altogether unexpected – I am, after all, British, and there's nothing we Brits like more than having a regular whinge about our weather...

Our son Daniel *loves* freedom and space. He loves being outside in the sunshine and fresh air. Whiling away hours on his beloved trampoline is probably his favourite pastime, whether it be for bouncing purposes, dragging large toys onto it, chewing the safety netting or simply lying back and sunbathing. He loves visiting the local park or playground, so he can lie on the swings, or inappropriately climb up and then block the slide for other users. He loves running around on the grass, particularly when trying to evade and dodge the responsible parent or adult who's trying to catch him – Aww, the beaming smile on his face when he's dodged a lunging adult for the fifth time! You can see how much he loves it. Equally our girls love playing outside. Only this afternoon, Rebecca saw a slide show photograph on our computer taken a few years ago, of a rare occasion when we had used the mini-blow-up paddling pool. She looked at me wistfully and said, "Daddy, one day do you think we'll be able to set that up again to play in?" "Hopefully... one day," I responded.

So *why on earth* do we continue to live in Britain? It has to be said, this year has seen the worst winter anyone can recall for years. We've all seen as the TV weather presenter gleefully announces in front of their display that we've broken even more records than usual for dullness, coldness and blanket cloud cover this year. For around six months every year, we Brits put away the lawn mower, the gardening tools, and the outdoor toys. We collapse the table and stack the chairs, and retreat behind our closed doors and double-glazed windows into the safety and warmth of the interior, and remain holed up for the duration. When we do go outside, the procedure has clear parallels with Neil Armstrong's EVA on the moon. An hour-long, carefully planned "suiting up". The only thing missing is a depressurisation of the "cabin" (a.k.a. front hallway) before cracking open the door to the front porch.

Now I am extremely fortunate to have visited my brother Rob just this February in Delray Beach, Florida, just an hour's drive north of Miami. By a miraculous coincidence, a work-related conference was taking place at the "Pan-Am International Flight Academy" in Miami, and I managed to sneak a couple of extra nights to visit Rob. On Rob's road during those two days, I was able to wear shorts, t-shirt and sunglasses, and sit outside on the front porch watching the world go by. Absolutely magnificent!

The only similarity I can come up with right now between Florida and our place here in Crawley? I'm thinking of launching airboat tour rides (Everglades style) in our back garden. Goodness knows the lawn is boggy enough, and who knows what wildlife may lurk beneath the waterlogged surface... The difference? I recommend full wet-weather gear and thermal undies for my tour...

So, Daniel and the girls will have to hold on just that little bit longer this year. Keep going with the spinny disk, bouncy balls and toy box (literally... the toy box... not its contents) for just for a few more days or weeks. The shorts, sun lotion and t-shirts are poised and ready... after all, we don't want to miss the whole summer do we...?

...And having said all of that, today the great British weather has stuck two fingers up at me, and it has been warm and sunny all day!

Stim City

In the world of multi-sensory output

Living with an individual on the autistic spectrum really makes you question human behaviours and their acceptance within society. A common association with autism is the stim. To explain, the stim or stimming is the name given to repetitive movements, sounds or activities carried out by the individual. A few examples of stimming include hand flapping, toe walking, rocking and head banging, but the list goes on. Stimming is more prevalent in those on the autistic spectrum but ultimately it is a behaviour found in all of us. It is often seen as a way of receiving a positive sensory feedback or to distract from a situation that would otherwise have a negative response in the individual. Imagine a scenario where a person is startled by an unexpected noise. They start to rock because they find the sensation of rocking makes them feel better, and as such it relieves the anxiety caused by the noise.

So, the stim doesn't really sound like a negative action. Well yes and no. It depends on the behaviour. If it involves self-harm (head banging), danger to others (biting) or is deemed inappropriate (stripping), then yes it has negative consequences. However, stimming can also be a natural coping mechanism and help encourage positive behaviours. To some degree, we all stim, particularly when scared or anxious. Anxious toe tapping waiting to go into an appointment, nail biting? We go about our business unaware of our own stims and equally most of society would also be oblivious to them. However, those on the autistic spectrum or with developmental delays may have more pronounced, exaggerated stims that make them stand out from the crowd. Rocking is one such movement that draws attention.

Daniel's appearance alone does not make him stand out from the crowd. If we were out in the street, his appearance alone would not attract any attention (although he is rather handsome – bias). The fact that we usually have a tight grip on his hand might, but more noticeably, his gait is not typical. He will toe walk in situations or walk with an uneven stride, particularly in situations where there is a lot of activity going on or he is uncertain of his surroundings. This is not a physical limitation. He can walk in a regular stride and oh boy, he can run fast!! At the same time, his vocalisation will become repetitive groans or if happy/excited a loud 'Aye'. Continuously observing, he will hold his arms out loosely, with his hands limp as if ready to flap. In more tense situations, Daniel will lightly head-butt your arm, with increasing force if anxiety levels are rising. Evaluating a situation, Daniel may remove himself mentally while remaining physically planted to the spot. By this I mean that he can look vacant as if he is a world of his own. Most likely, for that moment, he is and will be processing what is going on around him before deciding whether it is a settle, fight or flight situation.

If Daniel were to venture out in to the big wide world on his own – it's not going to happen but IF – then almost certainly he would be ridiculed, bullied and in danger. These coping mechanisms would almost certainly lead to trouble and sadly, not really through no fault of his own. He is communicating at a very basic level his feelings at that given time. This all comes down to balance. As parents, we have a duty to Daniel to try to develop a set of life skills that allow him to communicate safely. However, we also need to recognize that he has sensory needs that must be met in order for him to cope with the stresses of everyday life.

This is where we need to not point the finger and laugh, or worse attack, for you wouldn't survive without your own stims.

Those Strings You Pull

From Mother to Son

Dear Daniel

Nine years and six months of age (almost), 140 something centime-tres with the darkest brown eyes, lightly tanned skin, full of muscle ex-cept a slight pizza belly and a heart-melting smile, you will always be my baby but oh boy you are getting big.

On the way to respite yesterday, you aired your grievances in the car. This wasn't a typical Sunday journey and this wasn't what you were expecting. The tears ran down your face, transition always so tough. Mummy held your hand, trying to soothe away the anxiety. By doing so I noticed that your little hands are not so little and your head can now nearly rest on my shoulder. Yesterday handholding wasn't helping and the frustration imploded into head banging and hitting out. These outbursts are not as frequent as they once were but as you have grown so has your strength. In the midst of hitting you will look at me, full in the eye, with a pained expression, seeking for me to put right whatev-er is wrong in Daniel's world. Those who think eye contact in someone with autism is non-existent need only watch you for a day. Your eyes communicate all your emotions and more so when you make contact with someone willing to read them. As Mummy watched you walk off with Daddy, the numbness from my bruised arm was as apparent as the anguish on your face.

Once safely inside, the anxiety passed and the familiar surroundings made you feel safe, secure and happy again. Sadly, life is full of detours, unscheduled stops and throwing caution to the wind, something that doesn't bode well for you. Yet, my beautiful boy, you have become so much braver in recent months, much more accepting of what life throws at you. Once imprisoned by your diagnosis, you now have a social calendar to envy and are living life to the fullest.

So then we turn to your little sisters. Those noisy busy girls who take your toys and disturb your calm. As much as we can see glimpses of affection pass between you all, equally we see that Daniel's world sometimes needs a break. Up until now, this has consisted of either Mummy or Daddy staying at home with you and the other parent taking the girls to go out. In recent months it has tended to be Mummy staying at home with you and generally I am fine with this, but just recently it has made me a little sad.

You see, Mummy spends a lot of time at home alone, now that all three of you are at school or playgroup and because I work from home. Admittedly I am working during that time but for the majority of the week, I do not see or speak to anyone during the day. It is not a grumble, far from it, it is what works best for us all but it can get a tad lonely. I may even take up a family tradition of talking to myself. Even your little sisters can now occupy themselves when they come home so unless they want feeding or are fighting, I do not get more than a few cursory grunts (7 is the new 13 I'm sure) from one and the odd fleeting request from the other. Then when Daddy comes home at night, quite often the evening is lost trying to persuade you little people that bedtime is quiet time and sleep is good. The remaining household chores and quite often more work prevails. Of course, we then know that we are not guaranteed any sleep because our resident night owl keeps us guessing every night, don't you honey? It means that weekend time is precious and in an ideal world we'd spend it together. Yet, it is the only time that you get to be Daniel, away from the routine of school and weekday activities and sometimes Daniel's world and that of the rest of the household do not meet in expectation. Sometimes the opportunity for time alone with you is wonderful, we will engage and spend some lovely 1:1 time together. Sometimes, though, you need that time out just being Daniel on your own little cloud, equally fascinating to watch, usually full of giggles and laughter but watched as an outsider from afar.

This is where respite is a godsend giving the best of both worlds. It means that as parents we can be united in an activity with the girls, knowing that you are off doing something you like doing without worry. Yet being a mummy, things are never quite that straightforward and even though I relish the opportunity to get out and about, my little boy is never far from my mind.

As in Disney's Lilo and Stitch, 'Ohana' means family and family means nobody gets left behind. It sticks in my mind and I struggle with it a lot. It can be particularly challenging trying to explain to someone why you have not been included in whatever it is we happen to be doing. I fear sometimes people think we try to hide you away. In reality, I'd like nothing more than to show off my beautiful boy. It can be so difficult in public when all three of you children are together. The need to protect you is so great.

Aside from the safety side, there is the emotional impact. People stare, be it out of intrigue or to poke fun, they stare and as you grow that increases. I no longer care for their glances but the flip side is that the world is a cruel place. I dread the day that one of your sisters comes home saying they are being picked on because of ignorance about their big brother. Whereas we can protect you from the taunts, unlikely to be going anywhere on your own, one day these little girls will face them in the big wide world. Rebecca is quite vocal at explaining autism to her friends and teachers, these days much more accepting of his condition, but there is still a desperately sensitive soul underneath. I can imagine it would only take one nasty comment to set her back.

The reality, though, is that you are never left behind. Since that positive pregnancy test in March 2004, you have been very much part of everything we stand for and the path we follow is led by you. Yesterday, your little sister bumped her head and required a quick visit to the walk-in centre at the local hospital. I recall taking you because you had taken it upon yourself to eat half a toilet air freshener. Also yesterday, rather bizarrely and slightly off-putting was the fact that the smell of uncooked part-bake bread rolls reminded of the early newborn nappies that we have encountered several times. Our first in everything, of course, I remembered the panic over your first soiled nappy. Plenty since heh Daniel!!

It isn't a yellow brick road we follow for sure but a journey that can only be your lead. The challenge for Mummy is to take a step back and allow you to take a slightly different path from the rest of us from time to time, meeting at the end, refreshed and content.

Love you lots,
Mummy

The Sunday After Respite

So I guess we looked like a typical family except Daniel was chewing on a chewy tube connected to a lanyard on his coat.

So it is now Sunday evening and our three children are in bed, not yet asleep, but it's still early. Order is restored and Daniel returned from respite this morning. We are very fortunate in that Daniel accesses respite, which includes a monthly overnight away from home so we can catch up on sleep and all those little tasks that stress him out. He gets to have fun lots of fun too during the time he is away and is settling really well. The only thing, as his mummy, is that I really miss him when he isn't home and for all the challenges he faces, I am always so glad to see him home safe and well.

I have noticed that as parents we never quite switch off. Last night, Daniel was still at respite and I had a minor panic when I looked in on his room and he wasn't there. I know he has a wonderful time and we need the rest but being off 'autism duty' always makes me a little uneasy. Never mind that the other two are making plenty of noise...

We are upfront that Daniel's challenges sometimes get us down and we are both lucky and grateful for the support we receive. Sometimes we are aware that we become absorbed in the difficulties autism brings with it and feel that we go on about it too much to those around us. It is true, occasionally we need reminding of the positives and that life goes on.

The problem is that there is that misconception that autism, ADHD and a number of other conditions are merely children being naughty, bad parenting, bad diet and the fact that there is often no physical impairment makes the condition invisible. There is an expected social etiquette that our son just doesn't conform to. All in all, we are still learning to live by the alternative rulebook. We don't expect people to give us preferential treatment or believe we are more deserving than others because of Daniel's problems. Indeed, both of us would very much like to blend into the crowd so to speak. All we strive for is that our children get the very best in life, and from time to time that involves swallowing our pride and accepting help.

Today, we took all three children to the local park. This would, I guess, be a typical activity that most families wouldn't give a second thought to. However, it has taken a long time for me to feel confident with taking all three children to the park. In the past, Daniel would have been safely strapped into a Maclaren Major but today he walked. We have a wheelchair on standby if we feel he may become distressed at any point during the excursion.

The problem lies with the issue that Daniel has no danger awareness. In the past, he has attempted to walk off a high platform on a climbing frame as opposed to going down the slide. Anyhow, Daniel set off to the park with Mummy and Daddy and his two little sisters. He held Mummy's hand and made no attempt to escape, lie on the floor or generally protest as we have seen frequently in the past. Daddy had hold of Sophie, who was much more wriggly and indignant about handholding, and Rebecca scooted off.

I mentioned earlier that autism is often said to be invisible but we are aware Daniel's gait isn't typical, he will often walk on tiptoes, he holds his arms in a way that his wrists are floppy but his arms are bent at the elbow (a little like the Zombies in Michael Jackson's thriller), his gaze may not be obviously focused and he can look a little vacant. On this particular trip out, Daniel has a 'chewy' attached to his person by a lanyard. The chewy is non-toxic rubber/plastic compound that he chews on. Chewing on something can often help disperse anxiety and provide comfort. Individuals with autism tend to have heightened sensory needs and chewing is one of them. This brought a few odd glances from children in the park. As Daniel has gotten older, we have had more people ask if he is autistic and we don't mind this at all.

Daniel climbed up a very tall slide with Mummy watching on the sidelines deciding whether she needed to follow. My heart was in my mouth because at the top of the slide were a pole and bars for getting down and I was not sure Daniel would figure out either. He chose to climb up the slide instead of using either and fortunately he used the same method to go down. At some point I am going to have to trust that he has learnt what to do but for now I will continue to treat him like three-year-old Sophie and shadow him. I am aware that I need to let him grow and explore but for all intents and purposes his developmental age is so hard to define and is much closer to toddler than his actual eight years.

Afterwards, we moved onto the swings. Daniel has recently mastered the grown-up swings after years of squeezing into toddler ones. The little girl next to us couldn't stop staring as Daniel chewed on his chewy happily swinging side to side. Daniel was safely led around the park by either parent, usually with a tightly gripped hand, as the other parent kept close guard on Sophie and an eye on Rebecca.

We then headed for the miniature railway. This is a sit-on rather than sit-in carriage and my fear is Daniel either trying to get off or leaning to touch the passing undergrowth. He instead sat quite appropriately with Mummy's arms around his waist.

And so to close, Daniel was excellently behaved, only a few head nudges in protest of going an unfamiliar route home. He even ignored his little sister's major tantrums upon being made to leave the swings. Now, the trials of a toddler's strops would warrant a chapter in itself.

I'm a Non-Celebrity –
Get me out of here!

Lines are now open. To vote, please call...

Channel ITV1 – All Day, every day

A new run of the six-times-a-year series that launched in November 2004. Non-celebrities attempt to survive two and a half weeks cooped up in a house with their two daughters and severely autistic nine-year-old son (in other words, the dreaded school holidays!). Watch as events unfold today, including disagreements, tantrums, food obsessions and fights. Can they survive the series and emerge as victors (i.e. with their sanity intact and house still standing)?

Yes, today, as Daddy writes this chapter, we have struggled to the halfway point in the current series running over the school holidays. But why have I not been voted off yet? (please!)

Seriously though, getting through school holidays with three kids is a logistical nightmare at the best of times. Getting through with annual leave is simply not an option – my modest provision of 25 days would already be exhausted before getting anywhere near the summer holidays. Besides, I'm not sure my sanity would survive it in any case! The relative tranquillity of the office is often a lifesaver.

Let's be clear – Daniel does not really thrive during school holidays. Like many on the autistic spectrum, routine is all-important. The school day gives the repetitive and predictable structure to Daniel's day that he needs. At school Daniel's teachers and support staff go out of their way to involve him in each day's activities, filling his time.

Equally, the girls, not so reliant on routine, have over-flowing reserves of energy during the holidays, which need to be managed.

At home our attempts to negotiate the logistics of surviving a school holiday whilst managing to fit in sufficient working hours by necessity often lead to a very fragmented and tiring existence – which, I hate to say, often deteriorates into something more akin to a "survival mode" rather than the amazing opportunity to spend quality time engaging with the kids that it ought to be. Sure, there are days when we encounter a surprise boost of enthusiasm and energy. Those days are absolutely wonderful when they occur. I wish there were more days like them. Is there a tablet or pill I can take perhaps that provides a quick-release "energy and enthusiasm" boost? On occasion I have taken all three children to the local park to play, taken my daughter for a full day out sightseeing in London, or ventured to a soft play zone for a few hours. But such days, as well as being financially draining, cannot realistically be sustained for full days or weeks in succession. So, in between split shifts, and days when the grandparents or babysitters step in to help, we grit our teeth, roll our sleeves up, and do our best to occupy them here.

And here we are right now then – at home... again. Daniel's attention span on any particular toy or activity lasts about five minutes at best. I often read about autistic kids who obsessively read one book over and over and over again, or watch the same "Thomas the Tank Engine" video back to back dozens of times. Daniel doesn't seem to have anything like that – or maybe he just hasn't found it yet? He, more often than not, flits between things for short periods before losing interest. Then he's back in the kitchen cupboards or fridge trying to forage for food yet again, or pouring out the contents of a full Ribena bottle across the kitchen cabinets and floor. Meanwhile the girls are bickering about whose turn it is to play with the spinning toy for the twentieth time. I've come in the kitchen and Daniel has run to the other room and started chewing the curtains. Sophie wants to go to the toilet. It's 9.30am and still about a thousand hours to go until the end of the day...

Amazing then, that this series of "I'm a Non-Celebrity" is in its 48th series and the people taking part are always the same, and no one has yet been evicted. All I can say is, it must be a hell of a success that it keeps getting renewed year in and year out!

Maybe at the end of it all, we'll be led through our front door by a C-list celebrity presenter, accompanied by fizzling fireworks and cheers from a large crowd, given a glass of champagne and a trophy. I suspect not... but hey, I don't care – as they say, it's the journey that's important... Honest...

We are not a Bah Humbug household but when Christmas approaches, proceed with caution...

Ebenezer Scrooge: I do not make merry at Christmas...

Anyone who knows Daniel well will say that for a fair percentage of the time, he is a happy, giggly, somewhat bouncy and mischievous young man. That is until; you deviate from his master plan. Of course, a lot of the time we have no clue what that master plan is but we know when we have overstepped the mark. Christmas involves a little forward thinking and we sort of know what to expect but there is always that curve ball.

So it comes to that time of year when festivities start and all little children are bouncing off the walls with excitement, right? Rebecca came downstairs complaining that she couldn't sleep on Christmas Eve. All perfectly understandable but she was in tears. The next thing we knew was that she was feeling nauseous, a recurring pattern. How do you explain that feelings are complex and that sometimes your emotions play a part in how you feel?

Yet, not all feel the excitement, some not at all and Daniel isn't alone. For those with a learning disability, who rely on routine to keep anxieties under wraps, Christmas is a real spanner in the works. It seems to start earlier and earlier each year and pretty much every aspect of daily life is altered in some way for the six weeks' build-up to Christmas.

To start with, he has his birthday at the end of November, again a non-event for him besides the fact that he did take some interest in his presents this year and was happy to play with them straight away... bar one. The thing that most impressed him, however, was a helium balloon. Simply give Daniel a room full of balloons or balls and he will be entertained for hours, no materialistic little boy here! The one present Daniel didn't take to straight away was a giant beanbag from Mummy and Daddy. The reason I suspect is that it involved

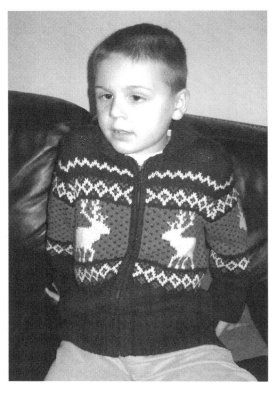

furniture being moved to accommodate it, and the crunch of the displaced beans as he was encouraged to sit down was altogether unexpected leading to a very anxious young man. Now that he has learnt what to expect, he has overcome that, preferring to bury himself underneath it and now just has to make sure those two other sources of unpredictability, namely his little sisters, are off it before he can fully enjoy it. Then, right at the beginning of December, there is another birthday in the house for his youngest sister. Now, he coped quite well with this, namely because there were more balloons and more importantly a second helium balloon. A pair of anything brings instant delight for Daniel.

And so, off to bed at night, expect to come down to the normal two slices of toast and a beaker of rice milk and notice immediately that all is not as it was the night before. There are twinkling decorations all over the house. In the past, this would have set off anxiety for Daniel but the one thing Daniel does like about Christmas is the vibrant colours, the twinkles as the decorations catch the light, toys playing Christmas melodies... over and over... and over and most of all lots of colourful lights. These days sensory lighting plays a part in Daniel's daily routine, 'sparklies' are not just reserved for Christmas so he is far more accepting because out of everything Christmas, this is something he can truly enjoy.

As you can see, not bah humbug, but sadly that is pretty much where Daniel's enjoyment of Christmas ends.

The ten things that stop the Christmas cheer in the eyes of Daniel and why:

10) Christmas parties – Daniel attends a lot of settings: school, play scheme, holiday club and respite. It is pretty much a given that all will have some Christmas festivity. As a rule, Daniel is happy to attend his placements, despite often meaning a change in routine or a visit to some place new. However, the one thing he doesn't do well is party (unless at home with his sensory lights). The increased noise, the busy to and fro really un-nerve him and he will do his best to retreat. We are fortunate in that, because Daniel only attends schemes that are either special needs or autism based, staffing provision allows him to dip in and out of events as he chooses.

9) Christmas productions – School begins to wind down and there is the annual nativity of Christmas event. As each year passes, Daniel's strength, size and Houdini methods of escape continue to outdo any engagements from his teachers to persuade him that it might be fun to go on stage... or stay upright on his feet if he makes it that far. If all is successful, it can be pretty heart-breaking as a parent to watch because it is evident from the haunted look in his eyes that he really has no comprehension as to what it is going and is more or less being a puppet... although the stage lights do hold their own appeal. Daniel is usually happy to go to school; it is very routine driven and he is familiar to the surroundings and his peers. This can change at Christmas because of the decor, increased number of visitors into school, and increased direct interaction with visitors (think large bearded man in a red coat and a trail of reindeer droppings). In the early years, the school's outlook was very much that everyone participates. However, over recent years, direction has changed and it is now only if the child shows real enjoyment that they are made to join in.

8) Santa and Christmas Carollers – A visit to the large bearded man, Santa? No chance. It includes waiting and going into an often confined strange place, both of which are a big no-no. Also, for a little man with absolutely no danger awareness, he does appear to have some stranger awareness and can be reluctant to go with anyone he doesn't know well. This isn't failsafe and equally sometimes he will refuse to go with someone he does know well but we aren't surprised to see him react in these circumstances. Currently in our house, the front door is cause for much concern. As soon as it is opened, Daniel becomes very upset. This can be if one simply takes the rubbish out. If someone comes in stress is quickly elevated and if one of us goes out, in equal measure. I am sure we'll get a few Christmas carollers so we'll need to be ready for that as it occurs.

7) Present wrapping – Step away from the cello tape if Daniel is in the vicinity. I remember, during one of our first house moves, trying to use packing tape with Daniel happily sitting on Dad's lap close by. You would have thought we were torturing the poor lad. Daniel doesn't like the noise of tape being pulled off, and this hasn't changed since that early episode when he was five months old. If we intend to wrap something or box something, Daniel has to be well out of earshot... which isn't easy because the boy has hearing like no other.

6) Christmas Snacks (and the not so edible) – Not bad in itself, lots of goodies that Daniel will eat BUT he doesn't understand the concept that we are waiting for this one big day or run of days, meaning that certain foods are 'in stock' but not for NOW. Daniel expects that any food provision he finds and is willing to eat is fair game. Last week, we had numerous mince pies, each with a bite out before being discarded. Ritz party boxes, Daniel will sit and eat in one sitting if given the opportunity. Daniel has added to the list by trying to eat the Christmas decorations this year. A few baubles have been stolen off the tree and none of them containing chocolate. This is a first and a very dangerous pre-occupation as one fabric bauble unravelled what appeared to be a cotton reel's worth of cotton and various chewed pieces of plastic. We had managed to Daniel-proof the living room in the hope that he could be left for a few minutes (only a few, mind) without chewing on something dangerous, stripping off, climbing the walls or escaping but have found that Christmas warrants for full supervision once again.

5) *Christmas visitations* – Christmas is the season when visitors tend to be more plentiful than other times of year. Although Daniel is overseen by lots of professionals and appointments/meetings fill a vast amount of the annual calendar, it is not the same as visitors who stay longer. Sometimes Daniel welcomes visitors with open arms and makes his presence felt by sitting squarely on them and making sure he has had his feet rubbed and cuddles. Daniel is a boy who likes to be pampered. Other times he will refuse to join them in the room. This is exaggerated in overnight stays because this often involves the girls having to share and a visitor being in one of the rooms. Daniel is very routine based and has the expectation that everyone will follow suit. If the visitor does not either follow said routine or similarly does something unexpected, it can lead to a meltdown. Overnight visitors are rare for this reason because Daniel's nights are very up and down anyway and the likelihood is that no-one will get any sleep.

4) *Christmas morning* – The saddest thing as a parent is watching Daniel on Christmas morning. He has not experienced any of the build-up that the girls have and the most important thing to him on Christmas morning is his toast and milk, as it is 365 days of every year. The girls are evidently very excited on Christmas morning and rightly so, but with it the volume goes up and the hustle and bustle of finding their presents can really put him on edge. We have tried to counteract this in recent years by allowing Daniel to stay in bed for a bit longer as the girls root out their presents. It is a bit trial and error because once he is up, normally he is wanting to be down those stairs.

3) *But I like my old...* – Daniel is very much a creature of habit and plays with a toy phone he has had since he was one. It is now battered and broken but it is a favourite. A second accompanies him to respite. Daniel used to really struggle with new toys. I remember one year we bought him something and switched it on and he burst into tears. A few hours later and allowed to explore on his own, he was able to discover it for himself with a much better reaction.

2) *Christmas Dinner* – This is the biggest challenge and one that we have only managed a couple of times with Daniel. Cooking a Christmas dinner at home takes hours if you are going to do it properly. Daniel expects that anything that goes in the oven will come out immediately for him to eat. With this in mind, he has learnt that his staple diet of chicken products, roast parsnips, pizza, and chips all take roughly the same amount of time, which is 30 minutes. To be fair, this is a vast improvement as he used to expect any tea on the table the minute he walked in from school. He will still whine and let you know his displeasure at waiting but has gotten better. Now, contemplate something taking two, maybe three hours including preparation and all hell breaks loose. Daniel will sit at the table the minute the oven goes on and will be very reluctant to move other than to look through the oven window to check what is in there. If, heaven forbid, you have to take something out of the oven and then put it back in again, this creates major drama. We have tried several ways of resolving the issue, such as trying to play with him in another room, letting him play outside, or letting him play in his room, but once he knows dinner is on its way, that is it. The only good thing is that once Christmas dinner is served, Daniel will usually eat it as long as he gets lots of turkey and parsnips, with the odd roast potato thrown in. He may still go and get the biscuits mid-meal.

1) Wrapping Paper – The opening of presents is Daniel's biggest fear at Christmas. You can see the anxiety building up as the noise gets to a point that he finds unbearable. Often he will retreat somewhere else and then let us help him open his presents once the girls have finished unwrapping. He will manage if the noise is controlled in the sense that he is involved or with you as you help him unwrap, but the sound of (usually) his sisters unceremoniously unwrapping as if about to embark on a world record becomes too much.

And there it is. As I read back, it does sound like we are very much controlled by Daniel and it cannot be denied that we are to a large degree. However, Christmas is an annual event and as such Daniel does not really get the opportunity to overcome or accept the challenges the holiday season brings upon us so we must do our best to accommodate. It can get frustrating because these things are meant to be fun and I am sure he would enjoy some of the festivities if not so consumed by the anxieties that overwhelm. All is not lost, though. Daniel accesses services that mean we can do all the Christmassy things with the girls so they do not miss out. Meanwhile Daniel is happy and well looked after, surely the most important thing after all – it is just a case of finding the balance.

If you read between the lines, there is a lot that Daniel does get out of Christmas and each year presents us with a fresh challenge to try to make it better than the previous.

Fighting Tooth and Nail...
(and Hair...)

Fear and Loathing

The severity of Daniel's autism may prevent him from partaking in many of the activities that so-called 'neuro-typical' children do as they grow. Daniel will never ask if he can pop out to play on his bike in the park. He won't go out for a kick-about with his friends from school. He'll never badger me for a few coins to run down to the corner sweet shop. It's unlikely he'll ever have a sleepover and watch action movies in his bedroom late at night...

There are some things he *can* most definitely do, however, as well as (or even better than) other boys his age – and that's grow, at lightning speed, impressive finger and toenails, continually sprout a thick head of hair, and grow (or lose) teeth, while being equally susceptible to the onslaught of plaque.

This, unfortunately, causes us something of a problem.

You see, Daniel most definitely does NOT like his teeth, nails or hair being interfered with. I guess you could say this about most children (and in the case of teeth and the dreaded 'dentist appointment', most adults too!) but Daniel's sensory processing issues, combined with his inability to grasp what is intended – or indeed, what is happening or why – take the suffering to another level, which can be extremely difficult to deal with.

Taking the dreaded hair cut to start with – and the infamous tale of 'Sweeney Todd' springs to mind. Think blood-curdling screams emanating through the door of the local barbershop... If they ever re-make a movie for Sweeney Todd, they would do well to record the shrieks and cries our little boy makes, to incorporate into the soundtrack!

In Daniel's younger days, the expedition to the local barber shop was a regular routine, as with most little boys, and he coped as well as you might expect – not always particularly happy or thrilled, but resigned to a few minutes of clipping and trimming with no particular problem. Around that time I recall Kirsty and me attending a local "Early Bird Course" run by the local council, which introduced autism and the problems we were likely to face in the coming years. During introductions by all of the parents attending with us, photos of our little darlings were shared – and one of the little boys, slightly older than Daniel, evidently had long, flowing locks of hair extending beyond his shoulders... "Wow, they should get that cut," was the thought on my mind, and surely others too.

Now of course... I get it.

Over the following few years, Daniel took a very clear and verbal dislike to the visit for a haircut. Kirsty and I don't particularly want to raise a male equivalent of Rapunzel, so we persevered with the regular trips as long as we could get away with it... you know, moving around to barbers in different parts of town, mixing it up, wearing disguises, keeping it unpredictable. Eventually they cottoned on – perhaps they networked, spread the word, communicated by text or code, closed ranks... "Hello... Frank, that little kid... Daniel... is headed towards your shop... thick hair... might be time to bail out, put the 'closed' sign up and lie low for a few minutes..."

Well, that part might not be entirely true, but we did reach a point where Daniel's distress, cries and screams throughout a hair cut in the very 'public environment' of a barber's shop were hard to endure and difficult for the terrified barbers.

Nowadays it's up to us... and our pair of trusty clippers at home.

Kirsty and I prepare stealthily, so as to try not to distress Daniel earlier than necessary. This involves positioning his wheelchair (with lap-belt ready to tighten) in the kitchen, and plugging in the clippers set to a 'number 2'... and just going for it as fast as we possibly can. We haven't yet had the police or social services show up to investigate the screams! Besides, within minutes of finishing, our boy is back to his happy, giggling, and now stunningly handsome self. All done for the next two months or so.

Trips to the dentist are, unfortunately, something we can never realistically attempt in our kitchen at home. Sure, there's a drawer full of numerous items of cutlery and kitchen utensils... but, well, just – no! The good news is that the local hospital is home to a dentist who deals with children with 'special needs'. No need to terrify the locals waiting in the already terrifying environment of the dentist's waiting room! Daniel is seen on a regular basis, and even sits in the chair... for a moment. You've got to work fast, though. Assuming you can get Daniel to open his mouth at all, the best you'll get is a few split seconds to try to glance at as many teeth as possible (and whatever you do, don't insert any fingers).

Actual treatment is a far more serious prospect to deal with. There is simply no way that Daniel will willingly open his mouth long enough to endure a brush, scale and polish, clean, tooth extraction or fillings. Unfortunately, the only way to undertake such treatment is to schedule a general anaesthetic in hospital, and carry out as much treatment as possible within the one visit. It's a big deal any time a child has to undergo a procedure under general anaesthetic, and something we have only suffered once during Daniel's life so far. But there will surely be further work in the future, and this is something we do not relish.

...So, the final of the three, the dreaded finger and toenail trimming. And this is an activity firmly in my own court as Daniel's dad! (I am the designated family nail trimmer for all three of our children!). And you know what? Our boy actually copes with this fairly well! Perhaps there is a 'sensory element' to this that is actually relatively pleasing (or rather, less distressing) than the other two activities? Who knows?

It's not that I ever have to cut my own fingernails after all. There's far too much stress dealing with my children's issues for me to seriously hang on to my own nails for long!

Bedtime Live

The only sleep experts I know are the ones fighting it.

So it has come to light that there is currently a programme where parents can receive help live on TV from a sleep expert and we just happen to find ourselves watching it.

Having finally managed to get all three children to a) stay in their own respective bedrooms, b) stop irritating each other through the plasterboard, and c) run out of excuses why Mummy and Daddy must come upstairs now – is this really suitable viewing?

Bedtime in our household is a chaotic affair that the younger members of the family most certainly rule. There is Daniel, who has a very unsettled sleep pattern and for whom bedtime is not always a favourable time. However, for the purpose of this post, we are using "happy" Daniel as example. Daniel will usually go upstairs with minimal fuss and cooperate for getting ready in his pyjamas and having his teeth cleaned. This is his routine and he knows it well.

Daniel has a "tough furniture" bed that is basically a giant soft play block. On top of this he has a standard spring mattress. In Daniel's bedroom is little else other than his bed and some favourite toys. He has shutters on his windows and no light. Furniture has been gradually removed following climbing escapades and clothes being used for chewing comfort. Sadly, poop issues have also been an issue and subsequently the room is "easy clean" as much as it can be.

Anyhow, Daniel's bed is not a bed for the first hour. It is a giant slide or climbing frame and is skilfully moved into precarious positions designed to give maximum scare factor to Mummy and Daddy as Daniel plays at Batman and Spiderman and hangs upside down. He warbles quite happily, at the same, independently moving his bed for his indoor playground. After a while we hear a change in mood and note that he is probably ready for bed and would like someone to reassemble his bed. Daniel has melatonin to help him sleep so usually has this and then gets tucked into bed. This generally is NOT the last we will hear from Daniel, even on a good day.

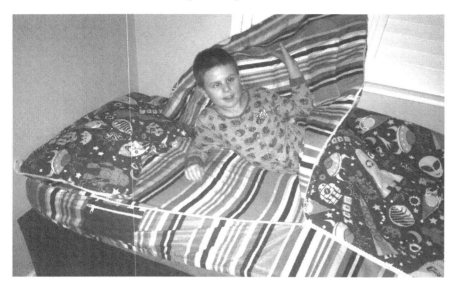

Next door to Daniel is baby sister Sophie. Sophie has a gate on her door suited to her toddler age. She is also toilet training. It is fair to say the two do not mix and Sophie uses the need to go to the toilet to escape from the confines of her room... frequently. As a typical three-year-old, Sophie is assisted to get ready for bed and brush her teeth. However, to potty, Mummy and Daddy are kicked out of the bathroom and she has learnt, much to our despair, to lock the door. This is thanks to her big sister. Sophie likes to take her time getting ready, which quite often involves streaking around naked and finding anything else that distracts her from the task at hand. Once pinned down and safely in her pyjamas she will expect a bedtime story or two, three, four. Then she likes her lights just so, her music on and if she can get away with it, her sister to play with her for a few minutes. Eventually she will let one or both parents leave her in her room but quite frequently there will be calls to downstairs: "Mummy, I need a wee wee", "Daddy, I want piglet". The once-quiet Daniel can often be awoken by such protests and then we have "unhappy" Daniel to deal with.

Rebecca on the other side of Daniel is much better at going to bed. She is independent for the process but does get very aggrieved that both Daniel and Sophie are assisted to get ready. She is a good girl though and very capable. That is except for being quiet. She is mummy to Lilo kitten and he shares the room with her at bedtime. This can lead to giggles as she plays with him or chases him around the landing after he escapes during one of her visits to the toilet... or like her sister, one of the numerous calls she feels the need to make to Mummy and Daddy. Rebecca's excuses are much more elaborate with her concerns about going to the dentist (appointment not for four months) or she will find a reason why she just needs to pop downstairs. Oh and did I mention slamming doors? Rebecca sometimes does acknowledge that her brother and sister are asleep and will creep to the toilet but will ALWAYS slam the door. This can trigger a disgruntled Daniel further, whom we then discover needs a nappy change. As we set him down in the bathroom, a little voice from the neighbouring bedroom shouts, "Mummy, I need a wee wee" and then a door slams...

A few hours after bedtime we settle down to watch the TV and we choose to sit through Bedtime Live, umm... we can at least sympathise.

Man on the Moon

Sometimes, acceptance is all that is needed.

During the period of writing this, sadly our family suffered bereavement, but out of respect for those involved I will not dwell too much on that here, except to say that we have lost someone extremely special.

Daniel was not party to the goodbye ceremony or wake, as sadly he would have understood little of what was going on and most likely would have found the situation too foreign to his usual activities. I did find myself sitting at the wake, wondering whether anyone wondered why he wasn't present or noted his absence, as often he isn't at family events. This got me thinking about how much we do include him in activities that may fall outside his comfort zone.

There are blogs we follow with children of similar levels of functioning within autism and they have made the conscious decision to include their child in everything in the hope that exposure will desensitise them and thus anxiety will no longer be an issue. Initially I would say we were very much in agreement with this viewpoint, and in the early years Daniel accompanied us to everything. However, it became apparent that it is not always obvious what is at the root of Daniel's anxieties, and with two younger siblings to also cater for, sometimes it is better not to disturb him from his comfort zone.

As Daniel and his siblings get older, I feel we have become more confident in taking Daniel out and as a family, dog walks and trips to the park are now feasible, although not always without drama. There are some situations though where you have to let Daniel be. Yesterday, we were all meant to attend a family meal, a pretty important family meal as well with family from overseas, a rare opportunity to be together. We had had the conversation a long time before as to whether

Daniel could cope with this and had made the decision that, as he is very much a 'fast food' kind of guy (as in, if he is hungry you have less than 30 seconds to find him something), this particular meal would be a step too far. With childcare arranged, the rest of us were due to attend, when last minute the carer could not make it. Then ensued half an hour of deliberating as to whether Daniel could actually cope or if we had time to arrange something else.

It was finally decided that I would stay home with Daniel. The meal was important to all involved but there was a strong chance that Daniel wouldn't have been able to cope and the repercussions would be lengthier than the meal itself. We have learnt that unhappy Daniel means unhappy pretty much everyone around him. So, Daniel stayed home with Mummy and was fairly chilled for the afternoon. Mummy was obviously sad not to be able to see everyone but we had at least managed to catch up the day before, with Daniel present.

Daniel attends various activities that see him having to face up to situations he may not be particularly comfortable with. As time goes on, we hope that we also will be able to include him in more activities, meals out, etc., but there is also this balance where we need time to spend with the girls, where we do not need to rush through a McDonalds because Daniel has become pestered, or our walk to the park is a little more leisurely and 'off route' whereas Daniel needs to be taken the route he knows.

Today, it is the first day of half term. Daniel has a day at his respite centre because we have building works in the house. I was fretting because he wasn't due to leave until 10 and the builders were due to start at 8. The generators have been running pretty much since 8:30 and drilling since 9. Daniel didn't seem bothered initially by the men in the garden, although he did choose to close the curtains. However, when I got up to take him, he was upset to find the noise outside extremely loud and the car not parked in its usual place. This really did bother him and his reaction was to lie down in the middle of the path and cover his ears. Fortunately, with a little bit of encouragement, we made it to the car but he remained unsettled for the journey and into the centre.

It is difficult. As with any child, we cannot wrap Daniel in cotton wool, so he will have to be exposed to things he does not like as part of development. However, we also have to be aware that some things that we may simply view as unpleasant, he may find excruciating, means of torture and extremely frightening. Senses in individuals with autism can be heightened to such a degree that simple tastes are overbearing, or they can be desensitised to the point where they do not realise they have hurt themselves. It is important to view any difficult situation with this in mind.

With this in mind, Daniel is very much part of this world, our world, our lives, always with us. However, he has his own little world that sometimes he needs to escape to. We are still exploring Daniel's world, like the man on the moon.

Wait and See

Daniel does not, as a rule, do diversions, deviations from the route, or detours. Today, Daniel surprised us.

Wait and see how Daniel is... this is something that we might say when planning an activity that could include him. Plans are often last minute because of this. Today was a classic example.

Today Daniel had part of the day with Daddy. Mummy was at work and the girls were with Grandma. Mummy took over with Daniel later on as Daddy went to the dentist. Daniel, having woken in good spirits, became inexplicably upset when Daddy went out. There were proper big boy tears rolling down his face.

The conclusion was that he too wanted to go out, this after attempts to pacify were limited, snacks gratefully received but not enough to deter Daniel from his uneasy moan. I had to go and pick up something from a shop on the other side of town, a route that Daniel rarely frequents. There I was contemplating whether a trip out was what was needed here but at the same time realising that I could be playing with fire.

Daniel does not, as a rule, do diversions, deviations from the route, or detours. Today, Daniel surprised us.

After the tears, Daniel quite happily jumped into the car... always a good sign but the happy sounds continued even though we took a left where we would normally take a right, then on down that road where Asda is but we were not going there.

And so this continued right up to said shop and then right back to the traffic lights close to home. However, Mummy turned right instead of carrying straight on... a few anxious grumbles could be heard from the back of the car. However, within minutes we were parked.

Daniel was still a little uncertain and gave me a little tap on the shoulder, as if to say 'I am not sure about this'. However, as I said 'park, Daniel' he spotted it and the happy sounds returned.

A wonderful twenty minutes or so were spent exploring. Daniel loves play areas so this isn't unusual, is it? Well, yes he does love play areas but usually only ones he is familiar with. This was in a different part of town, new route, no familiarity.

Later on, back home and after Daddy had returned, the three of us set off to McDonalds. This is a favourite for Daniel and it was fairly quiet so no trouble there. Outside, it was suggested we pop into the DIY store, about 200 yards or so away.

Normally we wouldn't contemplate this. Daniel does not tolerate shops well nor does he like to walk in unfamiliar places. However, with Mummy and Daddy holding one hand each he quite happily skipped across the car park. He then tolerated a walk around the shop quite happy to hold hands, not attempting to run off or drop to the ground, just quiet and content.

All this and it is the holidays, so well done Daniel. If only there were fewer stares from others, mainly I think because Daniel is getting big for hand holding, but if you have something precious you hold it tight.

It Started with a Missing Beaker

Daniel has a special beaker. A Tommee Tippee Kids On The Go insulated one. It is discontinued...

Every now and then we will check out the toddler section in the supermarket and spot one of 'Daniel's beakers' and manage to build up a supply 'just in case' one goes astray. Well, yesterday all three were missing. One lives at school, and normally two reside at home. One went AWOL during an outing. The other went to respite on Sunday and went to school with Daniel on Monday. It didn't come home... no beaker!

The boy was not happy! He cried and banged his head hard on the table. Who knows what the neighbours thought? Mummy tried to call school, the respite centre with the wailing continuing in the background. Seriously you cannot come between boy and his beaker! We have had real battles to get Daniel to drink outside the home. There has been limited success with children's disposable juice bottles but ultimately the beaker always wins. This was the first time we had been without one at home. Never be complacent where Daniel is concerned!

Today, another drama... the school bus, half empty due to most of the school being involved in a production, arrives home early and by a different route. Daniel does not take kindly to this. Nor does he like the decision to stay home with his PA instead of going out to the park. Just to reiterate this discontent he resorts to hitting out and not allowing his poor PA anywhere near.

For the past few days, Daniel has barely touched his dinner. The sunny weather and the call of the trampoline might be the reason but the vigorous chewing on the trampoline net, the evident stims and slightly vacant stare tell another story.

Autism in its full spectrum of colour, or is there more to it?

The Easiest Tough
Decision I've Made

Travelling on business to Seattle in 2010. When the taxi arrived to pick me up, our whole family was enjoying an afternoon of summer's day fun in the garden. I'd been bouncing with Daniel on the trampoline... and then within a few minutes I found myself hauling a suitcase out the front door, and leaving everyone behind. I hated that, I really did.

As I write this, I find myself in a quiet hotel room, alone, some six thousand, six hundred miles from home. Six thousand, six hundred miles from my wife, my son and daughters, their everyday activities and achievements – their laughs and stories, petty fights, bickering, messy rooms... their smiles, cuddles and kisses. Daniel's happy warbling and requests for extra drink, his very vocal annoyance when dinner is not prepared instantly. My daughters' pleas of "Daddy I want a cuddle!!" when I walk through the door each night from work ("I said first", "No I did"). All of this, reduced to a series of pixelated images transmitted to a screen halfway around the world, via text, Facebook, FaceTime or email. This, together with some lovely reminders that I brought packed in my suitcase... two beautiful felt tip pictures from the girls, and an engraved compass that was a gift from Kirsty, with the words *"Dear Mike, my love travels with you, Kirsty"*.

As I sit here in Singapore tonight, I know, however, that there are only four more nights until I arrive back home – and that this is my "final mission" away from home, at least in the current job. After an incredible 23 years and 10 months, I will hang up my flight simulator engineer boots for the final time as I count down the final few weeks in the office (and yes there *are* actually boots... they have steel toe-caps, and are a health and safety requirement for the rare occasions that I might work underneath a flight simulator).

This comes about following a request for application for "voluntary redundancies" at work approximately one month ago. And despite never having done anything else since finishing further education in 1990... I felt the strangest sensation – I felt myself thinking "actually, maybe I should go for this".

Rewind to October 1990. "Show me Heaven" from the movie Days of Thunder by Maria McKee is at number one. I remember the Daily Mail headline being "Major the Meteoric" as John Major superseded Margaret Thatcher as the British Prime Minister, and the first Gulf War was soon about to kick off... And I put my smart shirt and tie on to start work at what was then Rediffusion Simulation, in Burgess Hill.

For a single, just-out-of-University twenty-one-year-old, the work was amazing. And the opportunities for travel spectacular. Within seven months of joining I was off to Hong Kong for over ten weeks. The following years saw me despatched to far-flung places such as Atlanta, Tokyo, Denver, Zurich, Frankfurt, Brunei, Shanghai, Miami, and Memphis, to name a few... all subsidised by the company to work on Flight Simulator installation and local qualification. The work was always hard and the hours long, but with no family of my own and no attachments at home, it didn't matter. You could say this was my "gap year" (or years), my "travelling the world when I'm young" phase... with the incredible bonus that I was in fact working and being paid for it!

Things change – life changes – and nothing stays the same forever. I had always wanted a family, to find "the one" as it were – an amazing woman to share my life with, to build a home with, to have children with and settle down with. As I saw each of the various sights and sounds at exotic locations around the world, I found more and more I was niggled by a need to share them with someone, not just alone. When I found Kirsty, everything changed. On the very eve of my site trip to Sydney in 2002, I broke down and cried at the thought of twelve weeks away from her, even though I knew she had arranged to see me at the midpoint of the trip. And in fact, my carefully considered plans to propose on one knee at sunset outside the Sydney Opera House were abandoned, as I ran upstairs to unpack the ring and propose there and then in the cosy living room of my house that final night. On the next long trip to Frankfurt in 2004, I followed the progress of Kirsty's first pregnancy (with Daniel) via phone calls and emails, returning home with around one month to go. Everything was changing as each year passed, and more and more I hated to miss any of it.

Travelling on business to Seattle in 2010, when the taxi arrived to pick me up, our whole family was enjoying an afternoon of summer's day fun in the garden. I'd been bouncing with Daniel on the trampoline... and then within a few minutes I found myself hauling a suitcase out the front door, and leaving everyone behind. I hated that, I really did.

Site trips are not the same when you have a home, a wife, a family waiting for you. Travel is not the same alone as when spent with those you love in the next seat. As I've been writing this in my hotel, I have my mobile phone here at my side, my eye always half on the screen wondering if a text or a message might come through. Singapore is an incredible place, a thriving city full of life, amazing sights and sounds and colour, there's no doubt. But as I experience each aspect of it, I find myself wondering whether Kirsty would like this, or the girls like that, or Daniel like that. This is my mind set.

I agonised over the decision on voluntary redundancy for some time. The opportunity had not been one I had expected to open up, for one thing. Nor was I sure they would accept my application. The job is also one I have absolutely loved doing, and been passionate about, there is no question about that. So why should I not then follow the age old showbiz mantra of "leaving while I'm on a high", or "always leave them wanting more"? Fear was probably the major blocker in my mind. Fear after nearly a quarter of a century doing one job... the expression *it's all that I know* comes to mind. However, this thought was always followed by that of – do I really want to do just one job for all of my working life? I think I should be bright enough to find something else, after all... shouldn't I?

It's the desire to return to home... and stay there... and be there each night with Kirsty, and watch my three children grow up, and not miss anything (they are all still under ten years old. It's not too late!!) that clinched it. At work they say they want to reduce the amount of site work – in a world where money is tight, and computer links, the internet, video conferencing and WebEx allow a great deal of remote working to exist, that will be possible – to an extent but not completely.

I know with my whole family's support, I can get through my fear of finishing this job and finding something else. Maybe something completely different? Hopefully equally as interesting and enjoyable? Then move as a family into the next, hopefully wonderful, phase of our lives together.

So really, leaving was the easiest tough decision I have ever made.

The Blessing of
the Little People

It has finally sunk in that with three children, two dogs and two cats, the house is going to suffer some wear and tear and... it could be worse.

Since the arrival of our firstborn, Daniel, I have been a working mum. I am still a working mum but the difference for the past couple of years is that I am a stay-at-home working mum. We have said goodbye to the last of the lovely people who had watched the children for us as we both went out to work, moving on to pastures new. The recession saw my career resemble something of a roller coaster ride where it changed direction, stalled and then went full speed ahead. I am now settled in a job I love that I hope will continue to grow, that challenges and naturally generates enthusiasm. The biggest change, though, is that for the most part I work completely from home.

The benefit of this is that I am fully involved in our fledglings' lives, and with that I feel better about myself. However, it does have its downsides. I would describe myself as a quiet person who will retreat from being the centre of attention, but I do like to listen and observe, enjoy the banter and the atmosphere of the traditional working environment. Working from home can feel quite isolating in that respect because the canines that share the 'office' with me are not great conversationalists either.

If I am honest, if you had asked me six months ago about regularly managing our brood by myself, for relatively long periods of time, I would have been quite nervous. Such is the unpredictability of Daniel's behaviour, you can suddenly find yourself going from stability to long periods with literally no sleep and then when he does actually sleep, you don't because you are on high alert. You have to be mindful what kind of mood Daniel is in and whether it is safe for his siblings to play alongside him without fear of a swift head-butt or slap and then there are the pica tendencies (eating non-food items), inappropriate stims and general lack of danger awareness. The need for having a second or third set of eyes when really all your eyes want to do is shut. However, as I have mentioned we do receive some respite and for this I am eternally grateful because it means that Daniel gets to do activities he enjoys, the girls have some freedom to make as much noise as they possibly can (and oh they do), and we manage to put the house back together once in a while.

Equally, as the girls grow, their understanding of Daniel grows with them so I no longer have to worry so much about what they are doing around him. They know the warning signs and will move when they see a meltdown in the making. It doesn't mean they don't sometimes push him to the limits but to control their every move would be denying them all of a typical sibling relationship. With all things Daniel, there are new concerns that arise and new behaviours to manage but possibly because I am observing his daily behaviours, I feel more attuned to forecasting down periods, giving me more confidence to handle what occurs.

For years as a working mum, I have stressed about the state of our house. It has finally sunk in that with three children, two dogs and two cats, the house is going to suffer some wear and tear and... it could be worse. In the last month, we have changed from matte paint to silk in our hallway, in the hope of defeating the notorious 'pizza' and 'sweat and sour' trail Daniel leaves when he is too quick off the mark for you to smother him in wet wipes at the dinner table. Kitchen flooring has been the bane of my life for as long as I can remember. No mop, floor cleaner, steam cleaner or vacuum has ever managed to keep the floor tidy for more than three hours and whatever house we have lived in, the kitchen floor has been an issue. Oscar's pug fur appears to be static and stick to walls and skirtings. These days, though, the biggest sources of destruction are the girls, far outweighing the mess of Daniel and the furry friends combined. They can literally tear through the house leaving a trail of devastation, juice cups spilled over, paint on the table, cupboards emptied, jigsaw puzzles scattered from room to room, pen and stickers up the walls, in literally the minute your back is turned.

When I was out working, housework seemed to become a massive undertaking in which every room needed a complete overhaul each week, in fear that if it was left any longer, a small child could be lost forever in the rubble. Now, I am at home more often, so housework is a daily task. Once the children are at school, my paid job is my priority but I make sure little tasks are completely regularly throughout the day. Please be under no assumption that this means our house is spotlessly clean and tidy; it isn't and I gave up trying to be superwoman long ago. However, generally speaking, the children at least have their school uniforms laundered and ironed in a timescale that means there is no panic rummaging through the laundry basket five minutes before it is time to leave.

So, going back to being out of the hustle and bustle of a working life that follows a regimented routine. It does take some getting used to and I do miss it from time to time. If I look back though, say five years ago, when we were not receiving any support with Daniel and childcare was mainstream nursery, life was just a whirlwind of emotions. We were both having to leave for work early hours with two children, one recently diagnosed with autism and one barely walking, and place them in a setting where we were lucky if we knew the member of staff's name. Daniel had given up on sleeping and was extremely anxious a lot of the time. Rebecca was teething and because of the newly placed environment, prone to every cold and bug going, meaning we all got them. Having gone back to work part-time, to full-time, to full-time with overtime and Mike having to go on work trips, life was chaotic. This was the price for both of us having successful and well-paid jobs. It took me a long time to realise you really cannot have it all, or what you class as having it all really isn't.

I do get to see or hear from work colleagues, both old and new, fairly regularly, and the power of e-mail means you are never completely alone. The one thing I have discovered, possibly more so than anything, in recent weeks is that if you actually take time out to stop and enjoy time with your children, they are actually brilliant company. Sophie is at an age where the things she says bring smiles daily. Rebecca is at an age where she is learning and taking everything on board and then she likes to share that with Sophie in what becomes very similar to Chinese whispers. A classic this week was that Sophie told me that boys do not have babies, they have animals, like snakes, instead. The outcome of some of their conversations is hilarious as an observer. Daniel is equally as charming to be around... on a good day. Yesterday, I was driving Daniel home from play scheme and he was enjoying one of the songs on the radio and was quite excitedly jumping up and down on the back seat. All these things lead on to you appreciating the much simpler things in life and my children have always been absolutely precious to me, but I haven't really taken it in what they give back. Needless to say, they still drive me up the wall but that is just a given as a parent. There is the other side; our girls provide just as much drama as your typical office dynamics. The jealousy, underhanded motives and tactics adopted by little girls trying to get the one up on the other will serve them well when it comes to going into the place of work in years to come.

The danger of working from home is the risk of being distracted from a work task. However motivated you are, there is the risk that whatever else is going on might be less easy to escape if you are outside a typical working environment. There is the other end of the scale, where you become so engrossed that you do not switch off for work. With a child like Daniel, sleep deprivation and bedtime routine can eat into working hours. For this reason, it isn't for everyone. I am lucky in the sense that my previous jobs did involve some work from home, so I knew the pitfalls. I do have to be able to sit down and work hard but have learnt to not over-commit myself; you just end up letting people down. As I write this I refer to the statistic that says parents of children with autism find it harder to hold down a job due to the pressure and strains of caring for their child. This has been statistically proven and I fully agree that caring can be a full-time job in itself; however, this doesn't help those that are struggling to deal with the way their life has adapted... who want or need to work.

For many, the added costs of having a disabled child make working a necessity, but as much as anything work is a means of escape or avoiding isolation. In recent years, there was the real possibility that caring for Daniel would ultimately mean that I would have to give up working. We did discuss it; financially we couldn't do it and for me personally, right or wrong, I think I would feel a little lost without some outside work.

In recent months, Mike has joined me working from home and is currently embarking on his own complete career change. He is in the process of establishing his own business, which is very exciting but scary at the same time. The positive in all of this is that we can both take pride in what we do, continue to work hard but be more in control when things are tough with Daniel. Undoubtedly, those down periods are something we have to expect.

I guess one thing that remains a sticking point is what if it doesn't all work out. Well, it is a gamble, but after years of trying to make the hours work, the site trips for Mike, and the necessary overtime juggled with weekly appointments, reviews, assessments and general day-to-day challenges, we are lucky to be able to work at all. It can be very difficult to explain because for a lot of the time, the challenges are those behind closed doors. Autism is a full-time job and what were once our lifetime aspirations are now distant memories. Sometimes we need others to come on board and not look back.

What the future holds I do not know but as it stands, I have always felt that we will not let anything hold our children back, if we can possibly help it. By that I guess it means we also do not give in to circumstances that initially we think will defeat us, but instead look for a solution that works. Autism is a puzzle but puzzles have solutions and a better picture at the end.

Fear of the 4ft 4"

Regardless of size, a child full of frustration and their own inbuilt fears, with no concept of danger or strength, is a force to be reckoned with.

As a parent I never thought I would be scared of my own child and it isn't something that most would admit to. At 4ft 4" he was a good foot shorter than me and about a third of my weight. Yet, when that sparkle disappeared from Daniel's eyes, it was time to be very afraid. Regardless of size, a child full of frustration and their own inbuilt fears, with no concept of danger or strength, is a force to be reckoned with.

Daniel is quite a placid happy little boy but when he goes... he goes and his ability to switch mood has taken many carers by surprise. There have been times where we have feared that he is too 'autistic' for the local autism support group. Ultimately autism is a continuous learning curve.

Now, I love our little boy to bits irrespective of the challenges he faces but you cannot help but feel wounded emotionally, let alone physically, when subjected to an aggressive outburst of hitting or biting.

I wonder if there was any particular reason that the universal colour for autism is blue... hmmm.

Today is a blue day in our autism world. It started off pretty well; Daniel awoke in a reasonable mood and quite happily waited as I made his toast, quietly humming to himself. Then the school taxi arrived and since then I have felt, well, sad more than anything.

Sometimes, you can amble along quite happily. We accept that Daniel has issues and that is it, we are used to restrictions that we face in order to keep a sense of calm. We have adjusted and adapted and just go about our daily business, not really questioning that we are so different to any other family.

It was just Daniel, Rebecca and me for breakfast this morning, and everything was fairly straightforward. Daniel's taxi arrived on time and he compliantly let me put his shoes on and lead him to the taxi. There the mood changed.

It turns out Daniel is still really struggling with the journey to school in his new transport and I have known this since the beginning of term. What really hit home today was the escort saying, "I am frightened of Daniel". I do understand why but at the same time that is heart-breaking to hear. This very same little boy has an infectious laugh, a beautiful giggle and a wonderful smile. I am biased as his mum but also this is what others say about him... on a good day anyhow. As he has matured he has started to hit out more and it is a worry but what we see much more of is him self-harming by head butting or hitting himself and it is only when someone tries to prevent this that we see the lashing out. He does not bite, kick, scratch (although will occasionally pinch), pull hair or any other behaviours that are normally aimed at others. Yet, we still are pre-teen and as I fear what puberty has in store for us, it truly is a worry that a fairly young child can overpower an adult.

As I face up to the fact that Daniel is frightening someone, I am conscious that others may also share this fear. The past two weeks alone, professional carers have said that Daniel has not allowed them to change his nappy or remove dirty clothing (socks). These are basic things we do several times a day without a moment's thought. We are lucky in that Daniel also has carers who are excellent with him and keep him on the straight and narrow, but the feeling is still there... no-one is completely settled in his company because he is so unpredictable. It is like constantly walking on eggshells.

There is the saying that words can never hurt you and in the world of political correctness, society tries to enforce this. However, words can hurt and today it is hurting. Tomorrow, I know I will reflect and learn because above all, at least in the case of the escort, she was honest. I need to know what the issues are so that I can resolve them.

All I can do is hope that sometimes, just sometimes, people see the little boy behind. There is more to this little fella than support plans, risk assessments, appointments and statistics. The little boy whose age is nearly double figures, will quite happily let Mummy play "This

Little Piggy" and "Incy Wincy Spider" on his arm to help him settle off to sleep.

He doesn't mind us blowing raspberries on his belly. It is only in those moments when you look into his big brown eyes, you will notice that his eyes are sparkling, for a brief interlude the dull vacant expression that autism often presents isn't there and Daniel will be fully focussed on you and what you are doing.

That is my little boy and the face I choose to remember. Autism remains a mystery unsolved and the biggest thing I would change for my son isn't necessarily his diagnosis, but that society can use it as an excuse not to try to discover the boy inside. There is literally more than meets the eye and they are not blue but the deepest chocolate brown.

I Get the Sentiment but it Doesn't Apply

Let's not start putting a stigma on disability.

Social media is full of quotes and aspirations to inspire and motivate us in everyday life. Every so often, one of these will be associated with special needs, or more specifically autism.

The sentiment often is that those with autism often just want to be accepted and should be allowed to live their life, not be labelled as an outcast. Absolutely, I agree, for some people with autism there is a strong feeling of wanting to fit in, a struggle with the awareness of being different and being a target for bullying. Society as a whole is too regimented that we all must fit into a 'type'. However, on the flip side of this, many people with autism do not possess the awareness or the cognition to give two hoots what other people think about them, let alone whether they are 'accepted'.

One such sentiment today that has hit a nerve is by Temple Grandin. In relation to the diagnosis of autism, the quote goes that the 'In the old days, diagnosis was gifted, not disabled'. I admire Temple Grandin and all that she has done to promote autism awareness and her experiences with autism herself. However, and the quote may have been taken out of context, this statement rings massive alarm bells.

For a start, the autism community has for years been trying to battle the stereotype that all individuals on the spectrum are 'gifted' with high intelligence and mathematical super powers. Those individuals are in a minority and are known as savants. Their talents and ability deserve recognition because it is RARE whereas autism, in all its forms, is NOT.

In the old days, unless I am very much mistaken, those with a diagnosis of severe autism, like Daniel, would end up in a hospital or asylum for the mentally ill. For those at risk of hurting themselves or others, a straitjacket would also be applied.

I do not see the struggles that Daniel faces daily as a gift to him. Usually, with a diagnosis of autism there are challenges that the individual must overcome in order to go about their everyday life. For us, yes Daniel is a gift, just the same as our other two children. We are fortunate enough to have our thought processes challenged daily, forced to consider another way of thinking, to explore human nature at its most raw and to question just about every ideal that society throws at us. That said, I would still prefer that my son didn't face the challenges that he does, and to make it clear that those that cause him pain are simply not welcome.

In a politically correct society, we have lost a lot of words that were once used to describe the differences in individuals. 'Retarded', for example, is no longer welcome. I am aware that there are those who do not see autism as a disability, including families with those on the spectrum. In recent years, Autistic Spectrum Condition has replaced Autistic Spectrum Disorder because apparently it is deemed more appropriate. However, for us who face the low functioning or severe end of the spectrum, disorder is more apt.

Let's not start putting a stigma on having a disability. All it means is that there is a limitation or challenge to overcome, and by raising awareness of such, you give the individual a much greater chance of succeeding than pretending it isn't there.

Off the Scale

Where exactly is Daniel on the scale, bouncing and flapping all the way along and back?

The Autistic Spectrum is often seen as a scale surrounding the triad of impairments, which are Social and Emotional, Language and Communication, and flexibility of thought, with higher functioning at one end and lower functioning at the other end. However, where someone 'really' appears on it, well, it's impossible to answer that question.

Daniel has a diagnosis of severe autism with a significant learning delay. This is also described as low functioning autism. As far as Daniel's ongoing abilities to live an independent life, the prognosis is low, and in terms of diagnosis, well, the 'severe' is there for a reason. He has strong impairment in all areas of the triad. He is unable to wash, dress, feed himself (with cutlery), use the toilet, read, write, be unaccompanied for any length of time, or communicate effectively, being non-verbal. On top of this, Daniel has an increased risk of developing epilepsy, particularly in his teenage years, with a ratio of 1 in 4 with a similar diagnosis going on to develop epilepsy. May I point out that this risk is not 1 in 4 people with autism, just that Daniel presents with a level of autism associated with this higher risk. The two conditions together decrease his overall life expectancy. Ok, so that is pretty depressing for a parent. Not only does our loveable little man present as a two-year-old in a nine-year-old body, he is at risk of other, quite daunting conditions and his life expectancy is lower than average.

It isn't good reading, is it? However, the point of this isn't to dwell on the negatives. It is to highlight that this condition is too complex to sit and wait, in fear of what we perceive might happen next. So, now we are going to look at the other end of the spectrum, with Asperger's Syndrome being the most commonly discussed high functioning type of autism. On paper, this is where you will sometimes find individuals who have savant qualities, have obsessions or strong interests, may appear socially awkward or withdrawn, but ultimately can learn to overcome their difficulties to live a reasonably normal life. I am, of course, skirting over myriad issues that affect both high and low functioning individual on the spectrum. This is my point. The term 'high' often leads people to believe there is little wrong while the term 'low' means there is lots. Well, for some people, for some of the time, yes, but life isn't that straightforward and autism certainly isn't.

For ALL individuals with autism, the autistic traits will bring some element of challenge to their lives. This isn't to say those challenges will not be overcome, but for the diagnosis to have been given, a trait recognised under the autistic spectrum must have been present. No one other than those affected have the right to say how much of an issue it is.

Here's the thing. Daniel sailed through the diagnosis process, mainly because of his failure to complete any of the tasks the paediatrician set for him. He gained very little speech in toddlerhood and subsequently lost it within months. At the time, Daniel did not respond to his name and eye contact was poor.

Looking back, the signs were there and on first reading up on it I can remember having that moment of realisation. For higher functioning cases that diagnosis can take months, years or never materialise at all, leaving the individual and their families to cope with a whole host of issues without any support. It isn't easy for anyone to get support but I do sympathise with the families where not having a diagnosis means you never actually get to the waiting list, let alone to the hand-hold at the end.

A lot of individuals on the autistic spectrum are regimented to routine. Daniel is not alone in having to have things a certain way, in a certain order, at a certain time and so on... Sometimes, this can be more explicit in 'higher functioning' individuals because they are able to have a lot more control of what goes on around them. With this ability comes more frustration, anger and anxiety when challenged. It is not uncommon for violence to be an issue with people on the spectrum. However, when you take someone with violent tendencies and a wide range of household implements that they KNOW how to use, you are dealing with a whole different situation. So in that moment, the anxiety and autistic behaviours in both high and low functioning people may mirror each other in terms of reaction and behaviour. However, the ability to act on them can be completely different. It is important to remember that resorting to violence is often out of frustration, and in both groups communication has failed in one way or another. However, we can see with Daniel the fight or flight process going on.

I could liken him to a frightened animal that needs reassurance and calm... and time. The cause for his upset is usually quite evident but sometimes the trigger can be a mystery. Yet, the brain is complex and even those who are able go about their daily lives independently can find themselves in desperate need of support with their own 'triggers'. However, the ability to ask for help might not be present in the severely impaired.

Cognitive ability has to play a part. Higher functioning individuals may have good or excellent cognition but severe anxiety and be trapped within their design to avoid circumstances that provoke. Daniel struggles with transitions but generally is quite accepting of new people and places. For every autistic trait that Daniel has, there is another that doesn't quite fit the 'typical diagnosis'. We broke the mould when we made him. J Where exactly is Daniel on the scale, bouncing and flapping all the way along and back?

So along the autistic spectrum, there isn't a pot of gold at one end, but there is a ray of colours with a whole host of individuals who need our support.

Education...
When Do You Stop Trying?

We are reaching a crossroads with Daniel's education.

Like most parents, we want our children to receive the best education they can. Alongside this we want them to be happy. Having one child in state special school and another in state mainstream, we are aware that the balance isn't always there.

Over the years, with Rebecca, we have had tears and tantrums that she doesn't want to go to school, no-one likes her, she doesn't have any friends, she doesn't like school dinners, she misses us when she is at school and the list goes on. Right now, she is happy, though, having settled into her second school and made some dear friends. She rarely fusses about going to school. Mind you, it has taken four years. Academically and socially, she is doing really well. She could put a little more effort into her homework but overall all she is doing brilliantly.

Daniel is generally settled at school but like Rebecca he has had a bit of a roller coaster of anxieties. He still struggles with transitions and the unpredictability of the other students, but overall he seems happy, and no concerns have been raised in recent months. As with everything Daniel, it could all change tomorrow given the uncertainty of what goes on in his mind, but if nothing else, he seems happy for now. So there we have it, Daniel is happy at school. We wouldn't want to change that, would we? Well, the concern is he is happy because he isn't being pushed out of his comfort zone and the only reason we'd want him out of his comfort zone would so he could experience new things... learning. Daniel's development has stalled for the past five or so years and although this has been accompanied by positives such as anxieties lessening, we fear that his communication and self-help skills are suffering. I have mentioned before that Daniel's receptive language is excellent to the point that sometimes you believe he understands all you say. There is the 'coincidental' laugh when we tease one of the girls, like Daniel gets the joke. The occasions when you go into a room and he will say 'hi' appropriately or 'yeah', that we have to dismiss in fear of getting our hopes up. Yet for Daniel to communicate back to you, he is reliant on gesture, facial expression or plain old meltdowns to get his point across.

The problem is Daniel presents as a child with severe autism, a significant learning delay and low IQ. Yet, there is a real sense that cognitively he can do and take on much more than he can express. It has been known that children who are non-verbal can read and type (not necessarily write if fine motor skills are affected). At eighteen months, Daniel could complete a shape sorter in a time to rival an adult. At three, Daniel could recognise his name from a selection at playgroup. I very much doubt that this method of testing has been applied to him since.

We attempted ABA Therapy around the time Daniel was four and initially saw an increase his attention span, eye contact and communication using PECS. However, once the intensity of ABA was left behind, Daniel reverted back. A similar thing happened with toilet training. Once the prompts were removed, regression immediately occurred and we have never regained toileting skills with him.

Daniel's school is brilliant in a number of ways and we're grateful that he is happy there. It isn't without concern though because educationally we feel he needs a lot more 1:1 time to progress; in fact he thrives on it. State special schools do not have the provision to provide the level of 1:1 to progress a child like Daniel. The sad thing is, if Daniel had been able to attend mainstream, with his diagnosis the chances are he would have been eligible for 1:1 support. He wouldn't have benefitted from any of the lesson content but hey, he would have had support. As the special school has so many additional needs to cater for – physical, cognitive, medical – there just isn't the possibility of providing the optimum in covering all the needs, not without more funding anyhow.

There are schools out there for autism and ABA schools that do work on the 1:1 provision with excellent results. The problem is that the placements are either like gold dust, far too few and local authorities make it almost impossible to get funding, or they are geared at higher functioning autism. This leaves a real dilemma for families like us who want the best for our child but cannot see any way they can obtain a fitting education.

We are reaching a crossroads with Daniel's education. We have raised our concerns with Daniel's current school, previously explored ABA options, and other SEN provisions. However, the battle to pursue those options is immense and, sadly, trying to cater for Daniel's everyday needs, we just haven't found the strength to forge ahead. That said, more avenues open with age and Daniel is approaching his 10th year, an age at which he may be considered more seriously for some of the autism specific schools. There are residential options that we have yet to consider that have proven excellent in providing a child with both the skills and structure they need to progress. Another year on and there will be secondary school options. There is still time, and yet, Daniel is happy at his current school so this at least gives us some time to make the right decision for him. It may be that he stays put until he is eighteen, the stability proving an important factor in his keeping his anxieties to a minimum and reducing the chance of other issues clouding over his learning potential. The increase in 1:1 is a must, but that involves amending his IEP and SEN Statement which is another minefield in itself and one I'll leave for another entry.

The hard truth about it is that the potential for a child like Daniel is deemed as low. As I have said, historically Daniel has been unable to retain any skill set without intensive support. I do get it but as parents will we ever give up hoping for better things for our son? The answer is no, for so many reasons. Daniel could have a breakthrough at any given time. He will never be too old for things to suddenly click for him. It is not unheard of for a non-verbal teenager to suddenly start to talk; rare, but not unheard of. We think Daniel understands basic sign language and as we intend to pursue this, if we are proven right, this is will be a massive breakthrough, however basic.

Any progress Daniel makes now will lead on to what sort of provision he will need as an adult, when we are no longer able to take care of him, so the investment now is critical. We want him to have the most fulfilling life possible, and assuming that he is not going to achieve, progress, and develop, and giving up hope, would effectively be clipping his wings.

The Traumatic Day we Thought Our Son was Gone... a.k.a. Daniel's First Tonic-Clonic Seizure

You think you have seen it all and then something comes along and shakes up your world... again.

For the past few months I've been slowly stumbling my way through "Breaking Bad" on Netflix. Anyone who watches this will be aware that this series often makes for compulsive yet very uncomfortable viewing. However, one device in particular used several times during the series is that where the 'pre-title' segment briefly shows a snippet of the very final scene of the episode first – usually something shocking and startling – leaving you wondering "Crikey – what on earth happens throughout the episode to lead to this?"

Here then is my Breaking Bad style "pre-title" sequence for this post. It's Saturday night (i.e. now), and what we see is that Daniel is in emergency overnight respite, our two girls are staying with their grandma, and Kirsty is being wheeled out of an operating theatre with her hand bandaged up following finger surgery... So what on earth has led to this? To find that out, we need to rewind a day and a half to Friday morning...

...And this I fear is going to be emotionally upsetting and uncomfortable to write. The events to come below happened just yesterday so remain very raw and very painful to re-visit. However, I feel it important for me to write this now with this still fresh in my mind. For anyone reading this who has a child with autism (or even without), who is unfamiliar in any way with seizures – NOW is the time to spend a few minutes READING UP ON THEM! It may never happen, but believe me, if your child has one and you haven't seen one before, it is a truly and monumentally terrifying event.

Back to Friday morning then – a normal school morning. We also follow a pretty predictable and well-oiled routine here on a school morning. Kirsty gets washed and dressed first. I come downstairs, empty the dishwasher, prepare Daniel's toast and milk for breakfast, then get him dressed and downstairs with his breakfast at the table. About now, Kirsty and the girls come downstairs so I head up to get washed and dressed myself. Nothing unusual at all at this point, and Daniel appears to be his usual self as I leave him to his toast...

Five minutes later, from the bathroom I hear a crash/bang followed by a lot of commotion. Something has happened, maybe an argument between the girls (not unusual here) or someone bumped themselves. But it doesn't stop – it gets worse... and louder... and I can hear screaming, repeated screaming. It's Kirsty and it's guttural screaming that I've NEVER heard from her before. I can hear it now as I write this and it's deeply distressing. I grab my dressing gown and run downstairs as fast as I can, the screaming just getting worse...

The scene entering the kitchen is my absolute WORST nightmare, so much so that it's upsetting me to describe here. My beautiful son, Daniel, is on the floor... and in that moment, basically appears to be dead... Kirsty is over him screaming his name. I grab him from behind to lift him up and he's a total, limp, unresponsive dead weight... to all intents and purposes, a body. Thinking he is choking (he was eating toast...) I do my very best to try to clear his airway, attempting in extremely shaky fashion the "Heimlich manoeuvre" and grabbing him around the waist and violently pulling my arms up to force anything out. But Daniel is a solid and robust ten-year-old, and as I keep trying this at the limits of my strength, at least a couple of times his forehead glances the floor... his arms are swinging loosely about. At the same time there is blood coming from... somewhere... It's dripping on the floor all over. Where is that coming from? I'm thinking 'my God, we're losing our son, no, no, no...' This is the rawest anguish I can ever recall as a parent.

Next I've placed him lying on the floor and at the same time this is going on, somehow I'm vaguely aware that the blood is from Kirsty's finger, which Daniel has somehow bitten down on, although this seems very secondary at the moment. I'm shouting at Daniel, shaking him and putting my own fingers in his mouth in case I can feel anything to dislodge. And by now, Kirsty has dialled 999 and we have the emergency operator online and despatching an ambulance and asking what Daniel's condition is.

The next thing I hear is the best sound one could possibly hear in the state we were in... Daniel making rasping and snoring type breathing sounds. He is still unresponsive but starts moving, and briefly opening his eyes in between periods of ongoing drowsiness and unresponsiveness.

Over the following minutes, Daniel, still extremely groggy and rather out of it, is breathing and trying to move – although I am now physically holding him on his side on the floor, frightened to let him move and indeed, under instruction from the operator to keep him in the recovery position as best I can until the paramedics arrive. This appears to take forever (although it probably doesn't – time doesn't pass at normal speed in such intense circumstances, after all). There's blood all over the kitchen floor and Daniel's clothes (again, from Kirsty's finger – but it adds some very unneeded drama to the scene).

Thank goodness they have arrived, they are assessing him, they are directing and helping and guiding us. There is a dressing rapidly applied at some point to Kirsty's finger to stop the bleeding. It's clear Daniel will be headed to A&E for further assessment, and while a stretcher is being prepared somehow I find a few minutes to head upstairs in a total daze and get some clothes and shoes on. Through all of this, the girls have been present and I have barely been aware of them, being so consumed by Daniel's predicament.

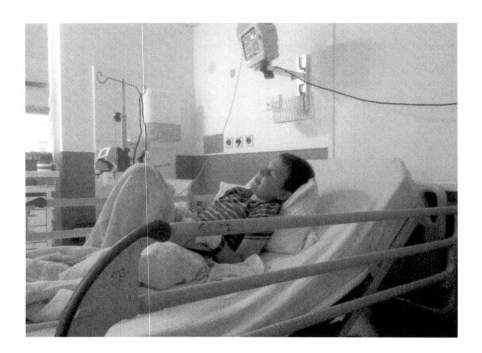

The Diagnosis

Our day continued for many hours at hospital, as Daniel was monitored at frequent intervals. And as the day wore on, an initially very
sleepy little boy very gradually returned to his more 'normal self' –
by mid-afternoon snacking on crisps and mini-cheddars on his bed in
hospital, and playing with some miscellaneous musical toys.

I also discovered roughly what had been happening in the minute
or two BEFORE I rushed downstairs that morning. Seemingly Daniel,
with no prior warning signs whatsoever, had narrowed his eyes and
basically 'paused' for a few moments, then toppled straight off his dining chair onto our hard (ceramic tiled) kitchen floor, later leaving him
with a nasty looking black eye. Kirsty, preparing school bags in the
hall, ran in to see Daniel convulsing on the floor – lying on his front
with arms and legs violently shaking. Believing he might be choking,
she lifted his head and desperately tried using her finger to check for
blockages in his mouth – at which time his jaw muscles contracted
involuntarily and clamped down on her finger hard, for some period
of time.

By the time I sprinted down the stairs, the convulsions had stopped
and he had become limp.

So we NOW KNOW after running through the events with the doctors and paramedics that this was very likely something called a tonic-clonic seizure, sometimes called a grand mal – a type of fit.

The following text is extracted from the "John Hopkins Medicine" website and describes pretty accurately what we saw with Daniel yesterday morning. Well worth a read, not only for this but for the descriptions one can find on the other types of seizures that can happen:

Tonic-clonic seizures (formerly known as grand mal seizures) can be one of the most frightening seizures to observe. There are two parts to a tonic-clonic seizure:

- *Tonic phase – The person initially stiffens and loses consciousness, causing them to fall to the ground. The person's eyes roll back into their head as the muscles (including those in the chest, arms and legs) contract and the back arches. As the chest muscles tighten, it becomes harder for the person to breathe – the lips and face may take on a bluish hue, and the person may begin to make gargling noises.*

  Many observers have the misconception that the person is in danger of "swallowing their tongue," so they attempt to put something in the person's mouth. Swallowing your tongue is actually impossible, and any attempt to open the now tightly clenched jaw may cause more harm than good. The tonic phase will typically last no longer than a minute.

- *Clonic phase – Typically following the tonic phase, the clonic phase will start as the muscles begin to spasm and jerk. The elbows, legs and head will flex then relax rapidly at first, but the frequency of the spasms will gradually subside until they cease altogether. As the jerking stops, it is common for the person to let out a deep sigh, after which normal breathing resumes. The clonic phase will rarely last longer than a few minutes.*

  As the person transitions from the clonic phase to the post-seizure period, they'll likely remain unconscious for a few minutes or more, depending on the severity of the seizure. During this time (known as the postictal period), the brain is extremely active trying to stop the cells from firing to bring the seizure under control. When the person wakes up, they may have sore muscles and be tired or confused. The observer's best course of action is to be assuring and supportive.

As I write this, just one day has passed since Daniel's seizure. We do not know whether this is more or less a "one-off" occurrence, or whether we will see further seizures. We obviously hope for the former but need to be prepared for the latter. We also currently await an appointment to discuss this with a neurologist in the near future. Being prepared and knowledgeable is our best course of action for now. By this morning Daniel appeared to have fully returned to his 'normal self', seemingly completely unaware of the fuss and concern he caused the previous day, playing with his usual toys and back in the kitchen with his normal healthy appetite for food!

Kirsty's Finger

It's clear now that Daniel was not choking – we also now know (amazing what you can learn online with the benefit of hindsight) that people who are choking will not convulse if they fall to the ground. And further, we know that under NO circumstances should you put anything... including a finger... into the mouth of a person undergoing a seizure, lest you want to risk either (a) damaging the object that is inserted, or (b) breaking the person's own teeth. The best action is to simply try one's best to keep the person away from danger during the convulsing phase, then place them on their side in the recovery position afterwards, and check that they are breathing and their pulse.

Despite the attention of the paramedic, Kirsty's finger had become infected following the nasty bite. During a follow-up visit to a surgeon at 11.30 this morning, she was unhappily surprised to find she needed to stay in for surgery to check the cut and thoroughly flush and clean the wound – a procedure requiring general anaesthetic and at least one night in hospital.

So here we are at the end of this traumatic episode... I managed to book Daniel into emergency overnight respite (with people well trained in seizure recognition and procedure), Grandma very kindly agreed to look after our girls overnight, and I stayed with Kirsty in hospital until she rather groggily re-appeared from the theatre tonight with her hand bandaged up.

I sure hope the next episode isn't like this...

And again, for anyone reading this, and particularly those with children who suffer learning delays or are on the autistic spectrum – please spend a few minutes reading up on seizures. I can't say it will make it any less scary, but any knowledge or mental preparation could be seriously beneficial if you ever experience one of these things...

When Lightning Strikes

They say lightning doesn't strike twice in the same place, but it does and frequently so.

From childhood, I have had a phobia of thunderstorms. When one is in the vicinity, I anxiously check the weather forecast, all my senses are heightened, my mouth goes dry and my heart rate increases. Anxiety sets in. My appetite goes and I can do little but focus on the impending storm. My body has pretty much remained in this state for the last seven days. There are no storms forecast. Yet there is lightning present, in the form of epilepsy.

This time last week I was on my way, by ambulance, to the paediatric accident and emergency department (ER) with my son. We had awoken after a reasonably good night's sleep at just after 8am. A lie-in in an autism household. Maybe that should have indicated that something wasn't quite as it should be. Three days prior, we had set up a sleep activity monitor that recorded any activity during the night, just so that we could observe Daniel following his first seizure. Daniel often wakes in the night so a monitor is useful irrespective of the potential for seizures. This particular night, the alarm mode wasn't set but as routine, I checked the longer recordings to make sure there was no cause for concern. Over the period of the night there were about five instances where Daniel was moving for two minutes or so. On the last of those, I was about to close the app, convinced it was just a rearrangement of the covers and a stretch, when there it was a tonic-clonic seizure captured at 4.17am.

Both of us ran straight to Daniel, who was fast asleep, breathing fairly heavily and obviously postictal. Postictal is the stage following a seizure where the individual is very sleepy, not particularly responsive and in recovery from what has happened. We made the decision to the call the UK service 111, where the operator asked us to check on some of Daniel's responses. Normally if we went into Daniel's room to get him up, he would be straight out of bed, ready for his breakfast. The operator decided that the paramedic response service needed to come in and check Daniel over. Within ten minutes or so, we were greeted by a paramedic who did all of Daniel's observations.

The UK guideline states that any child who has experienced a seizure must be seen by a specialist within two weeks. For Daniel this didn't happen, and his second seizure occurred two weeks and one day after the first. For this reason, the paramedic in attendance felt that Daniel needed to be seen in hospital, if only for the purpose of chasing up that appointment and so an ambulance was called.

After three hours in hospital, a rather upset Daniel was discharged from hospital, with a view that we needed to phone the consultant on Monday to pursue an appointment. All of that afternoon, he continued to be not himself, alternating between aggressive outbursts to very subdued and distant behaviours. By 7.00pm Daniel was in bed and 7.30pm fast asleep. This in itself speaks volumes as Daniel never goes to sleep this early.

Rather apprehensively that night, we went to bed early, a little anxious and stressed about what had occurred. The camera was switched on and the alarm set. At 3.09am, the alarm sounded and I saw that Daniel was mid-seizure. We both ran in and found that he was just coming out of the convulsive stage. His teeth were still clenched. Mike put him into recovery position, whilst I removed the cushions from his head. I then called 999.

Unlike the first seizure, two weeks prior, his breathing did not stop but was very noisy and croaky. He had bitten inside his mouth during the seizure and his lips had traces of blood. Both of us were very calm and able to speak to the operator without any issues. The ambulance arrived within minutes, followed by an emergency response car. The decision was made by the paramedics that Daniel would again have to go to hospital.

Daniel's younger sister, Rebecca, was home and woken up by all the commotion of the ambulance. Whilst Daddy went off, I tried to get her to sleep for a little while as she would need to come into hospital with me.

After the requisite time in A&E, Daniel was admitted to hospital, where he stayed for two days for CT scan, EEG and observations. Suffice to say it was all action stations and we were immensely proud of how well our boy coped. At the same time, he was formally diagnosed with epilepsy and started on medication.

So, Daniel is currently at respite but the past few days, with him at home, have been a whole whirlwind of emotions. The medicine has side effects that make him off colour. The risk of seizures remains high whilst he reaches his currently prescribed dose, and even then the dose may require adjustment. All the unpredictability is terrifying. As his mum, I am so frightened of letting him down and missing something vital.

The camera we bought has obviously been invaluable in that it made us aware of Daniel's plight. At the same time, it has changed from being quite cute, in that we could see Daniel bouncing happily on his bed, to something quite sinister. The alarm goes off with 'false alarms' due to Daniel being awake in the night. Each and every time panic is instilled. I hear the alarm when it is switched off, when Daniel isn't even here. I am trying to convince myself that we will be able to sleep again but it is early days. Unlike other conditions, epilepsy arrives 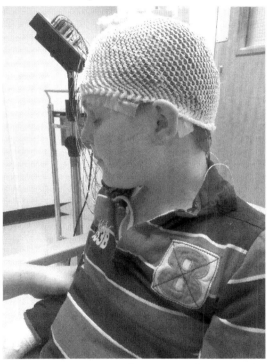 with a 'shock' and as Daniel's parents, we are still very much in 'shock'.

Whilst we have always known epilepsy was a risk for Daniel, the shock of it actually happening has been immense. Yet, we have been here before, a new diagnosis, a new journey with a long road ahead.

Printed in Great Britain
by Amazon

29894399R00117